QUEEN OF THE WOLVES

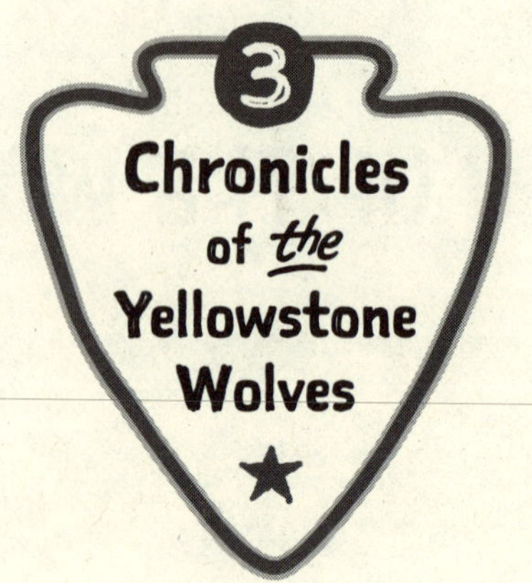
3
Chronicles
of the
Yellowstone
Wolves

RICK McINTYRE AND DAVID A. POULSEN

QUEEN OF THE WOLVES

The Legendary 06 Female

GREYSTONE KIDS
GREYSTONE BOOKS • VANCOUVER/BERKELEY/LONDON

For the Yellowstone
Wolf Watcher community.

RM

To my dad, Lawrence A. (Larry) Poulsen,
who instilled in me as a child a love
of reading that has never gone away.
Love you and miss you, Dad.

DAP

Contents

The Alpha Females

These family trees show you how the wolves you're reading about are related to each other. Because this book focuses on Yellowstone's incredible alpha females and the strong leadership traits passed down through generations, the family trees focus on those females (and won't show the other offspring born at the same time).

Druid Pack

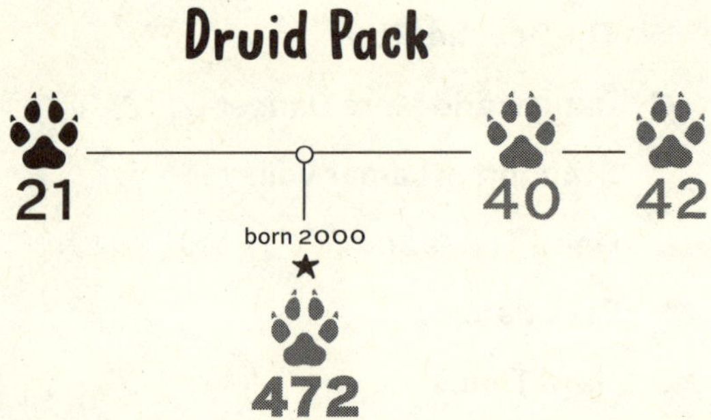

Although **Wolf 472**'s parents were 21 and 40, 40 died when she was very young. Wolf 42, who was 40's sister, bonded with Wolf 21, and they raised 472 together. You can read more about these wolves in *The Unlikely Hero* and *A Time of Legends*.

Agate Pack

The **06 Female** was Yellowstone royalty. On her mother's side, she could claim the legendary Wolf 21 as her grandfather and the equally impressive Wolf 42 as her great-aunt. On her father's side, her grandmother was Wolf 17, a sister to Wolf 21.

Lamar Canyon Pack

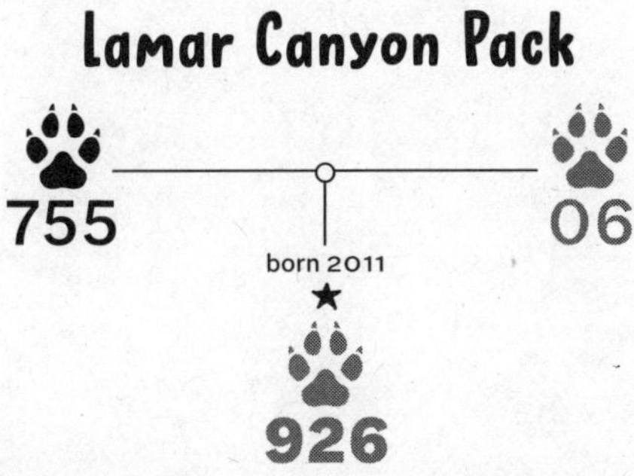

After the death of **Wolf 926**, her daughter—and 06's granddaughter—who was known as Little T, became the alpha female of the Lamar Canyon pack, carrying on the remarkable legacy of Yellowstone's alpha females.

A Lifetime of Studying Wolves

Rick McIntyre has devoted his life to the study of wolves. For more than two decades, he was part of the team of biologists, rangers, and park staff who studied the wolf population in Yellowstone after the wolves were reintroduced in 1995, and he continues to study and write about the wolves today. Rick grew up in a rural part of Massachusetts, and as a boy roamed the nearby woods and fields to be with and observe the animals he had already come to love. The more time Rick spent outdoors, the more he became interested in the wildlife he saw around him.

Rick studied forestry at the University of Massachusetts and, after graduating, continued to study the animals of the national parks in which he worked. But always Rick's greatest interest was wolves. As he came to know more about these amazing animals, he realized that wolves are the closest of all of nature's creatures to humans, particularly in the way they interact with and care for the members of their family.

After many years of watching wolves and chronicling their behavior in Yellowstone, Rick put his writing talents to work. He created a series of books designed to tell the world the stories of the Yellowstone wolves, including Wolf 8, Wolf 21, Wolf 42, and Wolf 302—four of the most famous wolves ever. Now Rick and award-winning Canadian author David A. Poulsen have teamed up to retell those stories for younger readers. In this third book in the Chronicles of the Yellowstone Wolves, they introduce the legendary 06 Female and other amazing alpha females. Together, these wolves demonstrate the vital role alpha females play in the pack.

No one knows exactly what a wolf thinks. But after decades of watching their behavior, the people who study these animals can imagine what is going on in a wolf's mind. Like their cousins, the domesticated dogs, wolves will often let us know what they are feeling and thinking through body language and sounds. No one knew the 06 Female better than Rick McIntyre, and no one is better able to convey what she and her daughter, Wolf 926, may have been thinking at any given time.

Rick's years of observations, gathered from watching 06 and the other Yellowstone wolves, are at the heart of this book.

Looking Back

The story of the Yellowstone wolves began in 1995 with the decision by the American government to reintroduce wolves to Yellowstone National Park in the western United States after an absence of almost seven decades. To do that, fourteen wolves in three different packs were transported from their home grounds in Alberta, Canada, to Yellowstone. One of those original fourteen was the runt of a litter of four male pups. That little pup, who became known as Wolf 8, was constantly bullied and picked on by his bigger brothers.

Despite his difficult beginning, 8 grew into an independent spirit. During one of his solitary rambles through the park he encountered the female Wolf 9, who had a litter of eight pups to care for all by herself. (Her mate, the pups' father, had been shot and killed on the very day the pups were born.)

Though still very young, 8 became the mate to Wolf 9 and the adoptive father to those pups. Almost immediately, he proved himself a worthy partner and father, and later would go on to become one of the greatest alpha males to ever live in Yellowstone.

But even great wolves experience their share of challenges. As the Wolf Reintroduction Project expanded, bringing new packs to the park, 8 faced competition. One spring day, not long after 8 and 9 had their first pups together, 8 spotted one of the new packs—the Druids—charging down a hill toward him and his family. In the lead was the huge and tremendously strong Wolf 38. 8 didn't hesitate: Though he was much smaller than 38, he ran straight at the marauders threatening his family and launched himself at 38. A dramatic fight ensued.

When it was over, Wolf 8 was the victor. But instead of killing his defeated rival, as is often the case when wolves fight, 8 chased off 38 to make sure the Druid alpha male wouldn't even think about coming back.

It was an amazing moment. The underdog not only successfully defended his family against all odds but chose to show mercy to his opponent. Courage and compassion were qualities that 8 would demonstrate over and over during his amazing life.

Young Wolf 21, a yearling at the time of the battle, watched his adoptive father as that battle unfolded. 21 was with 8 for two and a half years, and during that time was taught the lessons that would prepare him for when he became an adult wolf: how to hunt, how to raise pups, and how to fulfill an alpha male's responsibilities to his family.

Eventually, in 1997, the time came for 21 to leave his family and strike out on his own, just as 8 had done a few years before. Attracted by howling and the scent of one particular female—Wolf 42—Wolf 21 joined the rival Druid pack after the death of 38. There he raised 38's pups, echoing the actions of his own adoptive father, who had raised 21 and his siblings.

21 faced a major challenge when he joined the Druids: Wolf 40—the cruel and aggressive sister to 42. 40 had driven her mother and one of her sisters out of the pack, and had twice killed 42's newborn pups. Although 40's viciousness toward 42 continued, 21 seemed to have a rule that he would never harm a female wolf—even one as mean and violent as 40. For a time he tried to win her over, bringing her into playtimes with the pups and standing between her and 42 when 40 tried to abuse her much gentler sister.

All of that changed in the spring of 2000 when 40 once again prepared to attack 42's pups. This time, 42 was ready to stand up to her sister and fight for the lives of her pups. But she'd need help to win this battle. When 40 got the upper hand in the fight, two younger mothers—both of whom had also experienced 40's terrible temper and had always known kindness from 42, rushed to their friend's aid. Together, they overpowered 40. She suffered serious injuries and died soon after.

With Wolf 40 out of the picture, 42 became the pack's alpha female. Her compassion was evident as she quickly took over the care and feeding of 40's pups, a big job on top of looking after her own litter. Almost overnight, the personality of the Druid pack changed. The kind but firm, capable leadership of 42, coupled with 21's ability to protect and provide food for the Druid family, transformed the pack that had once been known as the "bad wolves of Lamar" into Yellowstone's most loved and admired family. And 42 was a shining example of the strong, capable females who played vital roles in every successful Yellowstone wolf pack.

1

The Battle

The female wolf was fighting desperately for her life.

She had been attacked and pulled down by three large males of a rival and quite vicious pack called the Hoodoos. The gray female, Wolf 571, was on her back and in trouble, but she was fighting with everything she had. Her little brother, a black yearling known as Triangle (named for a triangular white blaze on his chest), was trying to help by getting the three trespassers to chase him, but any relief he was able to provide for his sister was short-lived.

571 and Triangle were members of the famed Druid pack that had once been the largest and most dominant wolf pack in Yellowstone. Now, however, in 2009, five years after the era of 21 and 42, the Druids had been devasted by mange, a disease caused by mites that burrow into the wolf's skin to feed on fluids and tissue. A wolf with mange will scratch at the infected areas and

lose fur, making it difficult to contend with Yellowstone's harsh winter cold. The Druids weren't alone. Mange was running rampant in Yellowstone during those years, and many wolf packs were infected.

Earlier that morning, 571 and Triangle had spotted the three intruders near the place where two Druid pups were hidden away. Brother and sister were worried about the pups. They howled, and then charged at the trio of black wolves. The Hoodoos saw them coming and mounted a charge of their own.

571 and Triangle turned and ran back the way they had come, with the three big males in pursuit. The siblings split up and headed off in different directions. The Hoodoos ignored Triangle and continued to race after 571, who had been carefully leading the intruders away from the pups. She was running toward the nearby Lamar River and the park road. If she could get across both, her chances for escape would be much greater. But even though 571 was fast, the three males were faster—they caught her before she could get to safety. They were intent on killing her, as they had other Druids in the recent past. One of the three pursuers brought her down. 571 leaped up, counterattacked, and then took off again for the river. Three times the same scene played out, but on the fourth time, 571 wasn't as lucky. The three wolves fought the courageous female to the ground, biting her and shaking their heads, viciously

ripping and tearing at her. 571 was clearly in the last minutes of her life.

One of the attackers went for her throat, normally the final blow in a battle. But his bite was impeded by the tracking radio collar 571 was wearing, which bought her an extra moment or two. The Hoodoos quickly figured out what was going on with the collar, however, and one of the attackers repositioned himself to get at 571's throat from a different angle. He was eager to end this battle, which had gone on much longer than he and the others had thought it would.

Just as the Hoodoo was about to inflict that fatal bite, another surprise derailed the killers' plans. Triangle, the skinny little black yearling, leaped into the fray, intent on evening up the odds, at least a little. He darted back and forth, here and there, attacking first one of the big black wolves, then another. Chaos ensued, but only for a moment. Though 571 and Triangle were clearly courageous and quite skilled fighters, the battle couldn't go on much longer. Two of the Hoodoos teamed up and charged at Triangle, who took off heading east.

The distraction Triangle caused had allowed 571 to get up and resume her run toward the river. But the biggest of the three invaders ignored Triangle and pursued 571, catching her yet again. When the other two Hoodoos saw that he had her, they stopped chasing Triangle and raced back to rejoin the attack on 571, who, injured and exhausted, was increasingly less able to fight them off.

Once again, Triangle came racing to the aid of his sister. The three attackers were forced to stop and go after the little brother. 571, now closer to the river, was able to get to the edge of the water before the three black wolves got her again. This time, all four wolves tumbled into the river, with the three Hoodoos surrounding 571 and inflicting still more damage. That's when Triangle reappeared. He ran into the water at full speed and actually chased one of the much bigger wolves out of the river. Again, 571 used her little brother's distraction to her advantage. She finally made it across the river and the road, racing toward the safety of the Druid family's den.

Despite 571's successful escape, she had been seriously injured in the battle and was now sporting a massive, bloody wound across her chest. The three Hoodoo wolves, furious at the endlessly annoying Triangle, now turned their full attention on him. One of them bit his hind leg, but Triangle was able to jerk free. He was in pretty poor physical condition—the mange and now injured leg had left him quite weak—but he was somehow able to outrun the three Hoodoos and, like his sister, escape to safety.

But Triangle wasn't done just yet. The brave little yearling who had fought so hard to save his sister stopped and howled defiantly in the direction of the would-be killers before limping off in the same direction 571 had gone moments before. For the time being, at least, the battle was over.

The respite wouldn't last long. The next day the three Hoodoos returned to the area, perhaps intending to take over the Druid territory. This time, though, the Druid pack was back together at full strength. The Druid alpha male, 480, zeroed in on the biggest Hoodoo, the one who had inflicted the most damage on 571. The three intruders, a lot less brave when facing foes who might prove more difficult to take down than a small female and her even smaller brother, wanted nothing to do with the rapidly advancing Druids. They turned and fled, and didn't stop until they had left the territory.

But what of the fearless 571? Had she been able to survive the severe wounds she had suffered during battle with the Hoodoos? And what about Triangle, the courageous little brother who just wouldn't quit but who had been limping badly by the end of the fight?

Those questions wouldn't be answered right away. Neither 571 nor Triangle was visible for a while. Following the battle, they had taken shelter in some of the denser Yellowstone forest. The question that park rangers were eager to answer was this: Were they taking time to recover from their wounds or had they finally succumbed to their injuries? Several days went by.

And then, on a morning when the Druids were bedded down a few miles west of the den, Triangle was spotted lying not far from alpha male 480. All of the Druids were lying down, resting and partially hidden away in the tall grass. Finally, a gray female stood up, walked over to 480, greeted him, and pawed gently at his face. That gray female was 571, not completely healed but definitely on the road to recovery.

A few minutes later the Druids were preparing to move off. 571 immediately assumed the lead position. With hardly a look back she headed out, the rest of the Druids falling in line behind her. After they had been traveling for a while, the gray female finally stopped and looked back. She was surprised to find the rest of the pack struggling to keep up. The same determination she had displayed fighting the Hoodoos and protecting the newborn pups was evident again. She realized she'd just have to slow down to let the others catch up.

571 was a perfect example of the critical role females play in the life of a wolf pack. Not only are they the pack leaders and the bearers of the young each year, but they are willing and able to share the burden of protecting younger members of the pack.

A few years earlier, Druid alpha male 480 had led a charge against another, much larger, pack that had trespassed into Druid territory and were intent on doing harm. The only help 480 had on that day was a group of pups, who willingly followed their leader in the charge against those invaders. Wolf 571 had been one of those pups. When those Hoodoos came on the scene in 2009, 571 could have saved herself and run away. Instead, she charged at the three much larger wolves, intent on protecting the pups she was in charge of that day. She took on the role of acting alpha female and assumed the responsibility that went along with that position, proving the importance of the females in a wolf pack. ★ RICK

2

The 06 Female Arrives

It was nearing the end of 2009, and breeding season was just weeks away. The famed Druid pack was much smaller than it had been some years earlier, when it was by far the most dominant and important pack in Yellowstone National Park. It had seen its number fall to just eleven wolves: the alpha male 480, the new alpha female known as White Line, and nine young adults (seven females and two males).

But there was an even bigger and immediate problem. Wolves do not breed with close relatives, and 480 was related to all of the females in the pack. What was needed was an outsider male to come along, join the pack, and mate with White Line.

In situations like this, sometimes fate steps in and provides a helping hand. Early in December, a healthy (mange-free) male came along and soon was cavorting playfully with one of the Druid females. 480 came on the scene and, as would be expected, was not happy to see the new arrival. Even though he could not mate with any of them himself, his instinct was to chase off any new males that showed an interest in his daughters.

480 charged at the young black wolf, but the newcomer did not back down. He did, however, lower his tail to show that he recognized 480's authority. There was a brief standoff; then the fight started. But before the two males could get very far into their conflict, one of the females stepped between the warriors and the fight came to an end. The young females all knew that this new arrival was needed if the family was to have pups in the spring. Their father's actions were not helpful.

There were more skirmishes in the days ahead, most with 480 but even a couple with Triangle. But the black male stuck around, flirting with the female Druids. 480 tried without success to drive the persistent male away.

Readers will remember Wolf 21 and his ongoing, mostly unsuccessful, efforts to keep the handsome playboy wolf, 302, away from his daughters. The amazing story of 302, the bad boy who becomes a hero, is told in Book 2 of the Chronicles of the Yellowstone Wolves: *A Time of Legends*.

★ RICK

Eventually this newcomer was scent-marking around the Druid territory, an indication that he wanted to live in Lamar Valley with the Druid wolves. 480 had a decision to make. He would either have to accept that this new male would be part of the pack, or he would have to leave and try to find a new mate.

Just a few days after the arrival and eventual acceptance of the black male who would soon be collared and become known as Wolf 755, another new kid arrived on the block. But this one was a female—called the 06 Female. A beautiful, heathy, independent-spirited gray, she was not collared and had not yet been given a number by Yellowstone staff. Her official number was 832F, but her identity came from the fact that she was born in 2006. She was given that designation in part to differentiate her from her near-identical sister, born a year later.

When 06 arrived in Druid territory she was accompanied by one of her sisters and an unrelated male, but 06 had already shown that she didn't need a lot of company. She was a granddaughter of the famous Wolf 21 and the alpha female 40, one of the meanest female wolves there ever was. Both of 06's grandparents came from tough, independent, spirited stock, and it was clear that 06 had followed in those hardy paw prints. She spent much of her time as a lone wolf. Most lone wolves are males, but 06 was unique, both willing and capable of forging her own way.

Several male wolves had courted 06, but so far she had made no commitment and had not yet settled down to start a family. Perhaps she simply hadn't met Mr. Right.

◇ ◇ ◇

In the first couple of days after her arrival in the Druid homeland, 06 took down a full-grown elk on her own and then shared the meat with the two wolves who had been traveling with her. This newcomer was clearly an expert hunter and very capable.

On this occasion, 06 and her companions did not get to enjoy the results of her hunting prowess for long, as 480 and 755 put their differences aside and led the Druids to the kill, driving off the group of three that had been given the name Lava Creek pack. 06 retreated to the top of a nearby hill and looked down at the Druids feeding on the elk she had killed. It was the first time she had ever seen Wolf 755, and she seemed intrigued.

Once the other Druids had left the elk carcass, 06 and the little band of Lava Creek wolves returned to 06's kill and fed. Then, as she and her packmates moved off, she stopped, looked back toward the Druids, and howled. 755 returned her howls, and the two of them continued in duet. It was a sign of things to come.

Wolves are able to identify other wolves by their howls. Each howl has a main frequency, and then bands of sound that are different from that main frequency, giving each howl a distinctive pattern that is different from that of any other wolf. It would be similar to someone listening to a song by their favorite band and knowing from the sound of the voice exactly which member was singing. ★ RICK

The next day, there was one more encounter between 480 and 755 before the older wolf fully moved on from the pack he had been part of for so long. 755 and the other Druids had killed an elk. While they were away from the kill, 480, who had been nearby, began to feed on the carcass. Then 755 returned to the elk, and the two males looked at each other warily. 480 lunged and snapped at 755, but the younger wolf did not respond in kind to the aggressive behavior. When some of the Druid females returned to the carcass, they fed alongside their father while 755 bedded down nearby. It seemed that 755 respected the older male and went out of his way to avoid a confrontation.

After a while, 480 walked away from the elk carcass. It was the last time the wolf who had been a brave and capable alpha male for the Druids would be with his pack. He knew it was time to set off in search of a female he wasn't related to and perhaps start a new pack. He disappeared into the woods, never once looking back.

The Druid females—knowing that they needed a new, young, healthy male to take over the alpha role and revitalize the pack—welcomed 755 as the male successor to 480. It was a good plan. But only time would tell if it would work out.

3

The Last Days of a Great Wolf

It's not surprising that Wolf 06 was attractive to a number of males. She was a beautiful, healthy, strong, courageous female who would make a wonderful mate. Several males had recognized those positive traits and had certainly made their interest known to her. Although she had mated with a few different males, she had never had pups, and it was clear that she hadn't yet found the male with whom she wanted to share her life.

One of the males who she'd encountered was the one-time rebel turned responsible alpha male of the Blacktail Plateau pack, Wolf 302, whose life and journey had made him one of the most famous and beloved Yellowstone wolves of all time. 06 and 302 met when he was just establishing the Blacktails.

I have often thought about why so many people loved 302. He was an imperfect wolf, and that was what made him so relatable. The value of his life story is that in his final years he changed. We love stories about individuals who turn their lives around and become heroes, for they give us hope that we can also choose to do better. His story is told in vivid detail in the second book of the Chronicles: *A Time of Legends*. ★ RICK

It was February 2009 when 06 was dividing her time between the territories of the Druids and the Blacktails.

As the month wore on, the Blacktail alpha female, Wolf 693, had gone out of season, which meant she could not be bred. That was not the case with her younger sister, 06, and she soon found herself the focus of the three young males known as Big Brown, Medium Gray, and Big Black. 302 stayed close by, but the actions of the Blacktail alpha were very different from those of the three younger males. He was acting like a chaperone, protecting 06 from the unwanted advances of the over-eager suitors. Rather than pestering her in the same way the other three males were, 302 bedded down next to her, gently licking her back and placing his head on her as she lay there.

He let the young males know, with bared teeth, growls, and even by pinning them, that he was her protector. It was a different role for 302. He was attentive but not aggressive with 06. He was suave and caring. It was another example of the wolf he had become—mature, self-sacrificing, and willing to do what was needed to ensure the overall good of the wolves under his leadership.

It hadn't always been that way.

◇ ◇ ◇

The year was 2003. A large, young, black male appeared in Druid territory and immediately attracted the attention of several of the young Druid females, all daughters of the great alpha male Wolf 21. The handsome newcomer was 302. 21 immediately chased him and pinned him, and though he allowed the young wolf to get up and run to safety, the message was crystal clear: 21 and his mate, 42, did not want this fellow anywhere near their daughters.

The two Druid alphas were diligent but largely unsuccessful in their efforts to keep the very persistent and crafty 302 away from the young Druid females, who were almost as devious as the young wolf who was courting them. They kept finding ways to elude their watchful parents in order to rendezvous with the charming young stranger.

But while 302 was very interested in romance, he had no particular desire to take on any of the responsibilities that went along with fatherhood. His "love 'em and leave 'em" attitude led 302 to take off—ditching the ladies he'd so impressed, and leaving 21 to raise a number of pups that 302 had actually sired.

But it wasn't just his playboy attitude that made the early version of 302 a thoroughly unlikable character. He was also a coward, and more than once simply ran away from a fight to protect himself. In fact, during one such fight, he and his nephew were taking a beating from several Druids. Not only did 302 flee a couple of times, but he also did something even worse. When his nephew was pinned to the ground and being bitten repeatedly by their adversaries, 302 came running back—not to help his brother but to join the attackers in inflicting even more damage on him!

302 was a wolf who challenged the traditional roles of an adult male. The usual path for a young wolf was to seek out a mate, find an unoccupied territory, and set up a family dynamic, with the male taking on two main tasks: the hunting of prey animals that were often much bigger and stronger than he was and risking his own safety to fight off rival wolves that threatened his mate and their pups. 302 was unwilling to take on either of those roles.

Another telling example of his lack of character took place in the spring of 2007. 302, now a low-level male in the Druid pack, was resting alone near an old moose carcass at the base of Mount Norris. A rival group, the Mollie's, were nearby, much higher up on Norris—five adults and five pups. The rest of the Druids, nine of them, were about a mile to the west—adults 480 and 569 and seven pups. The Mollie's howled and the Druids howled back. Soon, a full-scale battle was underway. Leading the Druids in the fight that ensued was 302's nephew 480, who had by this point become a prominent member of the Druids and possessed all of the leadership qualities that his uncle lacked.

480 moved toward the Mollie's, with the rest of the Druids right behind him. But there was a problem: the group of pups he was with were not battle-tested and would likely flee when the serious fighting started. And start it did. Four of the Mollie's attacked, pinning one of the Druid pups. 480 charged to the rescue, with five pups following him. He chased and attacked one of the Mollie's adults, took it down, and then stepped back and let it go. While that was happening, the embattled pup managed to escape its attackers.

The battle raged on. Whenever 480 pinned a rival wolf, the pups would run in and bite the intruder. Due to 480's courage and fighting ability, and the willingness of the pups to get in there and do what they could, the Mollie's ended up leaving the battlefield in a hurry. Their anticipated easy victory eluded them. One courageous alpha male and several spunky pups had done what is expected of wolves—they had driven off enemies that were threatening their family and their territory.

302 had not engaged in the fight. Although he must have heard the howls between his packmates and the rival Mollie's, he never moved from his spot. He remained hunkered down near the moose carcass and let the battle go on without him as he fed and napped. It certainly seemed as though 302 would never be more than a cowardly, irresponsible reprobate who was loved by the ladies but wasn't much good for anything else.

◇ ◇ ◇

But then something happened. Not overnight, but slowly 302 began changing his ways.

In the summer of 2008, when he was eight years old—relatively old for a wolf—302 took a beating from three mother elk who had attacked him when he was trying to get at their calves. The big elk mothers stomped him; then, when he tried to get away, they caught up with him and stomped him again.

While recovering from the rough treatment he'd received from the enraged trio of elk, 302 and a couple of Druid pups hatched a plan to steal a calf carcass from a grizzly bear. After one unsuccessful attempt, 302 moved in close, and when the bear went after him, the pups dashed in and ran away with the carcass. Once they were safe from the grizzly, the pups settled down to feed. 302 bedded down nearby and let the pups have the meat.

Both of these behaviors were marked changes for 302, a wolf who had always been both cowardly and completely selfish. But here he was displaying a willingness to take a risk to acquire meat for his young packmates, and then being caring and respectful in ensuring that their needs were looked after before his own.

Was the old wolf changing at last? It certainly appeared that 302 was undergoing some kind of personality transformation. The question now was—would it last?

It wouldn't be long before that question was answered. Shortly after the incident with the grizzly, the Druids were involved in a battle with longtime enemies, the Sloughs. With 302 and the alphas leading the way, the Druids drove off the rival pack. The wolf who had always found a way to stay out of the fight—including running away as fast as he could—willingly went into battle alongside the other Druids. He proved to be both a willing and effective warrior.

But when the Druids returned to their home area the next day, things had changed. In fact, not all of the Druids made the journey back to Lamar Valley. Five yearling males remained behind. By late October it was clear that those five yearlings and a black female from the Agate pack had become a subgroup of the Druids—and that 302 was their leader. The subgroup briefly returned to the Druid main pack, and the Agate female returned to her pack as well, but not for long. Soon the five yearlings, who were nephews to 302, were again traveling west, with no resistance from other packs in the area.

The behavior of this group was unusual. Normally, young males will move off from their home packs one by one, seeking out one or more females in an effort to stake out a territory of their own. But this sub-pack seemed to want to stay together, and in mid-November, 302 and his companions, the five young males and five Agate females, were once again on the move.

One of those females was Wolf 06. She was beaten up and bloodied, the result of a confrontation with her aggressive sister, Wolf 693. It wasn't long before 693 and 302 began double scent-marking—a kind of raised-leg ritual urination indicating they were the alpha pair in this new pack. They ended up establishing a territory in a place known as the Blacktail Plateau. It was the very area 302 had grown up in as a Leopold pack member. The new pack became known as the Blacktail Plateau pack.

As the 2009 denning season approached, two of the Blacktail females, 693 and 642, were getting ready to have their pups. On one late March evening, with the sun dropping down in the western sky, 302 and the other Blacktails were bedded down in a pleasant meadow near the Blacktail Plateau. After a while, 302 stood up, picked up a big piece of meat he had hidden under his chest, and gave it to 642, who was just a few weeks away from having her pups. It was exactly the kind of gesture Wolf 8 and Wolf 21 had so often made with their mates, and it showed how much 302's earlier selfish personality had changed.

By late May, 302 was not only standing guard over the new crop of pups but was also busy bringing them food—racing off to feed on a nearby carcass and then hurrying back to the denning area to regurgitate meat for the mothers and their pups. Later that month, on a gray dull spring day, 302 was walking around the denning area that, nine years before, he'd played in as a pup. His once black coat was turning gray now, a sign of his age. After checking on the pups, and reassured that they were safe, he bedded down in a nearby marsh.

Not long after, mother wolf 642 set out in search of several pups who had wandered away and were now nowhere to be seen. She howled from time to time, but the pups did not answer. 302 finally stood up, stretched, and headed north. In a few minutes he had found them. As soon as the pups saw him, they rushed at him, jumping up on him and licking his face. 302 tolerated their enthusiastic greeting, then led them back to the safety of the denning site. He knew the area and had a pretty good idea where those pups would be. He took charge of the situation, and soon the pups were back safe and sound, their mother was stress-free, and 302, well, he could finally get back to that well-earned nap.

That summer and into the fall the pups grew into healthy, active young wolves. With 302 as their leader, the Blacktails were a thriving, well-run pack. It was also obvious that 302 was getting old. In fact, he had already lived longer than most Yellowstone wolves and considerably longer than almost any alpha male. But he was slowing down, often unable to keep up with the rest of the pack.

And there were new challenges for the Blacktails. A quota system was in effect for hunters who spotted wolves outside of the park boundaries: They could legally shoot twelve wolves who made the mistake of ranging outside the park. So far nine wolves had been taken, meaning three more could be legally shot.

Of course, there was no way 302 or any wolf could know or understand any of that. Park staff and all those associated with the Wolf Reintroduction Project in Yellowstone could only hope that park wolves wouldn't wander outside the park boundaries and put themselves in grave danger.

There was another challenge that the Blacktails *did* understand: A rival pack of wolves, known as the Quadrant pack, occupied territory not far from the Blacktail home area. So danger lay in two directions for the Blacktails—hunters to the north and rival wolves to the west.

On October 7, the adult Blacktails set out on a hunt. 302 didn't accompany them. He stayed back with the pups. It would not normally be dangerous for an old wolf and a group of pups, as long as they remained in Blacktail territory.

302 always liked spending time with the pups. And on this day, he was especially enjoying watching them play their favorite chasing game. He'd long been the super babysitter when he was a Druid. And now, as the alpha male of his own pack, he still relished the role. Unfortunately, on this occasion, things were about to go very wrong. 302 and his charges caught the scent of a nearby carcass and saw several ravens circling over the area. Unable to resist the temptation of an easy dinner, 302 and the Blacktail youngsters headed off in search of the carcass and eventually found it.

The bad news was that the carcass was in Quadrant territory. Soon after their arrival at the carcass, 302 and the pups were spotted by the Quadrants, who charged at them. Seeing the incoming danger, 302 turned and directed the young wolves away from the area, pointing them toward the safety of the Blacktail Plateau. The pups raced off with 302 at the back of the pack urging them on. It soon became clear that the Blacktails were not going to be able to outrun the Quadrants, who were gaining on them.

Realizing escape was impossible, 302 turned and faced the oncoming Quadrants, putting himself between the fleeing pups and the rapidly advancing enemy. It was a tactic his uncle, Wolf 21, had often employed to protect members of the Druid pack.

It meant the Quadrants would have to go through 302 to get to the pups. He braced for battle, ready to do whatever it took so the pups could escape. The fight was short. No matter how bravely and skillfully he fought, one old wolf could not hold off a pack of ferocious attackers for long.

But it was long enough. While 302 was giving up his life in a fight he could not win, the pups got away, ensuring not only their safety but the ongoing success of the Blacktail pack.

The renegade playboy who had been a failure in so many ways in his early life had more than redeemed himself in his later years. Not only had he become a responsible, capable alpha male and leader of the pack that he established, his reputation would live on after his death. 302 was much loved, not just by other wolves, but by so many people who had followed his journey and transformation. That journey ended with a selfless act of heroism in the final hours of his life.

4

06 Builds Her Team

There's no way of knowing if 06 was aware of the death of 302—the wolf who had treated her the way a kind, protective uncle might. While she'd spent some time with the Blacktail pack, and although she'd got along well with 302, she eventually moved on. Maybe it was because she wanted to get away from her bullying older sister, who was the pack's alpha female. Or maybe it was simply 06's independent spirit asserting itself. Whatever the case, she once again set out on her own.

◇ ◇ ◇

06 howled, waited a few seconds, then howled again. After a few more seconds, there was an answering howl. She was on a high hill, not far from the Druids. They interested her. Well, one Druid in particular interested her. The male Wolf 755, who had been hanging out with the Druid females after 480 left the pack, caught her

eye. Perhaps in some ways he reminded 06 of her father, Wolf 113, a nephew to Wolf 21. 113 had a calm, confident, and competent nature, and as a leader he avoided unnecessary battles with neighboring packs.

With the 2010 mating season only weeks away, 06's timing, if she really had taken a fancy to 755, was perfect. Was she finally going to settle down and have her first litter? In mid-January another young black male showed up and became part of the group. Though he was actually the bigger of the two males, he displayed submissive behavior to 755, an indication that he was willing to accept a secondary role in the pack. The two males seemed to get along right from the start, likely because the newcomer, who would be collared and given the number 754, was 755's brother. The two had become separated but now were back together. They were both healthy young males and were welcomed by the Druid females, who needed an injection of new male blood. But like his brother, 754 seemed more interested in 06 than in any of the other females.

Perhaps not surprisingly, 06 wasn't particularly welcome among those Druid females. All of them were suffering from varying degrees of mange, which greatly compromised their health. 06, on the other hand, was healthy and robust, and had all of her fur intact, which was so important during the frigid Yellowstone winter. Maybe that was part of the attraction the two brothers felt for her. The three of them were spending more and more time together. On one especially cold January day, they were bedded down together, clearly enjoying each other's company. When 06 got up and walked off, both males followed her.

It was an indication of what was to come. The three of them were soon doing a lot of scent-marking together, an indication that 755, 754, and 06 were forming a new pack that was given the name Lamar Canyon pack. 06 was four years old, and the two brothers were still classified as yearlings, making 06 twice the age of the male wolves she had bonded with.

◇ ◇ ◇

06 was alone. The two brothers were away hunting, but on this occasion she had chosen not to go with them. It wasn't long before another male wolf, known as Big Blaze, happened along and immediately took an interest in this fascinating female. Big Blaze was a former Druid and was now the alpha male for the neighboring Agate pack. He sidled up to 06, sniffed her, and was clearly intrigued. But 06 was having none of it. When she grabbed him by the throat—a potentially lethal move—Big Blaze wisely went into total submissive mode, and she released him. But Big Blaze was apparently a slow learner. He tried twice more to approach 06. Her reaction was the same both times; in fact, the final time he

approached her, she sent him packing, squealing in pain. 06 watched him go. She had made a decision: Her loyalty to the two brothers was real and not to be trifled with. From then on, Big Blaze stayed well away from 06.

Later that month 06 mated with both of the brothers. Around the same time, the last of the Druid females, a wolf called White Line, who was ravaged by mange, was killed by a mountain lion. Sadly, her death spelled the end of the great Druid pack, once the largest and most important wolf pack in Yellowstone.

The good news was that 06—who would soon be showing signs of pregnancy for the first time—was a descendant of the great Druid dynasty, so that line would continue and remain in the territory that been occupied by the Druids for so long.

It wasn't long before preparations were underway for the impending birth of 06's first litter. She chose an old denning site in an area once occupied by longtime Druid rivals the Slough Creek pack. Like the Druids, the Slough Creek pack had gone out of existence. The site was perfect for 06's first pups. Water was nearby, and there were lots of handy burrows for the pups to hide in when danger called. And there would be plenty of hunting opportunities for 06 and the two males, meaning a ready food supply for the pups once they graduated from mother's milk to eating meat. The one negative: grizzlies frequented the area. However, 06 had shown several times that she was not afraid of bears and was more than capable of dealing with this possible threat. She and the two males would have to be ready to face trouble when and if it showed up.

The weeks passed and the big day when 06 would have her pups was drawing nearer. One warm, sunny morning a few days ahead of her expected due date, 06 was in the den resting when 755 and 754 returned from a successful hunt. Excited to see them, she rushed outside to greet the two wolves. She knew they had brought her the meat she needed but was unable to get for herself because of her advanced pregnancy. She eagerly licked their muzzles, which triggered them to regurgitate the meat they carried in their stomachs. The adults would do the same thing for the new pups once they began to eat meat.

06 appreciated the brothers' dedicated effort as they worked to keep her and the coming pups strong and healthy. But she also knew that there were times when one or both of the brothers would try to put aside a little of the meat for themselves. This was one of those times. After 755 and 754 had headed back to the kill site for another load of meat, 06 came out of the den and sniffed around for a while. At last she found what she had been looking for: 754 had hidden away a cache of meat that he planned to come back for later. On this day, at least, his carefully laid plan did not work. 06 was too

sharp for that. She dug away at his buried stash. Then she lay down beside it and enjoyed a bonus meal, content that she had outsmarted her packmate this time around.

Finally, the big day arrived. 06 had her pups, and as is typical, she and the pups remained secluded in the den. After a while, she would leave the den to eat when 754 and 755, the pups' father, brought meat for her. But on May 9, she left the den for a different reason. A grizzly mother and two cubs had wandered into the area where 06 and the pups were denned. One of the cubs came to within 10 feet (3 meters) of the entrance to the den. That's when 06 charged out of the den and attacked the young bear. The mother grizzly came to the aid of her cub, but 06 continued to bite the young bear, and then dodged away.

Next, 06 turned her attention to the grizzly sow. She lunged at the bear, then dashed back to escape the reach of the animal's massive paw as it swung at her. She repeated that maneuver several times, and each time she drew the three grizzlies a little farther from the den and the pups. At the same time, she was making a high-pitched bark-like sound that was a call for help. She was hoping her two male companions would hear it and come running.

The bears became more and more frustrated as the battle waged on—with 06 continuing to taunt the grizzlies, dashing in, and then leaping back just outside the range of the giant bear paws. 06, on the other hand, seemed to enjoy the challenge. She had lured the bears well away from the den, and she wagged her tail as she confronted them again and again, a sign that for her, now that the pups were safe, this was fun.

For a time the bears left, and 06 returned to the den, but it wasn't long before the bears came back. Again 06 went through the process of luring the unwelcome intruders away. For four and a half hours the battle continued. At last, the bears became totally frustrated with this annoying creature that stayed one jump ahead of them at every turn. With a final unhappy look back at the female wolf, they finally wandered off.

But 06 wasn't about to let her guard down. She bedded down in a spot where she could spot the bears if they returned. And though she was exhausted from hours of fending off the unwelcome trespassers, she didn't sleep. She stayed awake and alert, ready to spring into action again at a moment's notice.

A few days later 06's pups came out of the den for the first time. Two males and two females, they were still wobbly on their feet. 754 and 755 both came to the pups and sniffed them, imprinting the scent of each pup in their minds.

If a member of a wolf pack gets separated from its pack, that wolf would be able to find the other members of its family by following their scent trail. A mother wolf quickly

learns the individual scents of her newborn pups. If one of them later wanders off, the mother can follow her pup's scent trail and track it down. ★ RICK

Not long after the brothers met the four pups this first time, a lone grizzly came into the den area. At first all three adult wolves lunged at the bear. Then 754 took up a position right near the entrance to the den, like a guard, alert and on duty. 06 bedded down nearby, and this time it was 755 who charged the bear over and over until the grizzly got the message and left. Once the bear was on its way, 06 went to 755 and licked his face as she wagged her tail. She was rewarding his heroism. And she was happy that the two males had shown both the willingness and the ability to protect the pups from any threat.

06 was a smart wolf, but apparently 754 hadn't figured that out. Returning from a hunt one day, he had an elk leg in his mouth. Once again, he deposited it in what he thought was a secret spot, then went to the den, regurgitated meat for 06, and spent some time sniffing the pups. Later, when he had left the den area again, 06 followed the scent of his earlier approach, found the elk leg, and enjoyed another bonus meal at 754's expense.

The pups continued to grow. They were healthy and, like all wolf pups, energetic and playful, enjoying endless wrestling and chasing games. It was mid-May, and 06 continued to prove herself an excellent mother, both as protector and provider. As the pups grew older, she was able to leave the den to hunt, and on one early-morning excursion she returned with a rare treat. She had killed a beaver, something that happened seldomly, as beavers usually stay close enough to water to be able to dive and escape a wolf. 06 placed the prize catch partway into the den, not only providing a treat for the pups but also keeping it out of reach of the two adult males.

Bears weren't the only threats that 06 confronted during that first spring of motherhood. One day she approached a golden eagle that was guarding an elk calf it had just killed. The eagle was perched over the calf, its wings spread over its prey. That gesture is called mantling, and its purpose is to keep other predators from approaching. But 06 was not afraid of the eagle; she quickly chased it off and grabbed the calf. But the drama wasn't over just yet. The mother elk returned at that moment and chased 06, causing her to drop the calf. For the rest of that day, the mother elk guarded her calf, but by the next morning she had left and so had the eagle. The dead calf remained where it had lain, with the wolves finally reclaiming their prize and taking it back to the den.

As spring rolled into summer, the pups continued to grow and thrive, while their mother again demonstrated that she was a unique female, both in her attitude toward other wolves and in her physical capabilities. That July she took down two elk, a cow and a calf, by herself. In both cases she had jumped up and made the killing bite on the throat. The cow had lifted her right off the ground but had been unable to shake her off, eventually succumbing to the attack. While other wolves were certainly capable of doing what 06 had done, they were almost always large males. 06 had proven once again that she could do anything that male wolves could do.

With the arrival of summer, the roles of 754 and 755 were evolving. Although 754 was the larger of the two brothers, he never challenged for the alpha role, instead becoming more and more involved in the care and protection of the pups. When the pack was traveling as a group, 754 most often stationed himself at the back of the pack, where he could keep an eye on the pups and make sure none of them wandered off or was endangered by a following predator.

In the games the pack members played, 06 and 755 enjoyed chasing games, though she was too fast for him and ran circles around the alpha male. Meanwhile, 754 played with the pups, romping with them and letting them catch him and even pin him down like they had beaten him in battle. It was like he was one of them. All seven of the wolves seemed thoroughly contented with their roles and their lives within the group.

When another grizzly wandered into the area while the adult wolves were away, the four pups, remembering what they had seen their mother do, boldly tried to harass the invader. The bear was not at all impressed by the miniature wolves. Realizing this, the pups slowed down their attack and changed their strategy. They followed the grizzly in single file, neither wolves nor bear particularly interested in pursuing the confrontation further.

As fall approached, it was increasingly clear that 06 was an excellent mother to her pups in the same way that her own mother, Wolf 472, had been to her. In turn, 472 had been raised by her aunt, Wolf 42, one of the most amazing mothers in the history of the Yellowstone wolves. A couple of generations later, it was obvious that the positive traits needed for an alpha female to be good at her job had been passed down from mothers to daughters.

5

The Second Litter

As summer rolled on into fall and the September leaves fell from the trees, 06 moved her pups into Lamar Valley. That meant that the Lamar Canyon pack, with its ties to the Druids, were now living in the same valley where famed Druids such as 21 and 42 had lived and raised generations of pups. The difference was that, at their peak, the Druids had numbered thirty-eight wolves, whereas the Lamar Canyon pack numbered just seven, with three adults and four pups.

One day not long after the move to Lamar Valley, 06 was feeding on a grizzly cub she had killed that had either gotten orphaned or separated from its mother. 755 was nearby, watching 06 eat. When 754 arrived on the scene, 755 blocked him from the carcass. But when 755 got a little too close to the carcass himself, 06 lunged at him and bit the alpha male. The two males had encountered 06's wrath before, when they had attempted to join her at a kill. As a result, they were now extra careful when she was feeding.

06 was in many ways an excellent mate, and she could even be caring and affectionate with the two males in her life. But she wasn't always willing to share meat with them. 754 and 755 had learned that lesson the hard way, receiving an occasional unpleasant bite from a female who was tough enough to take down an elk all by herself. Eventually she shared the bear cub carcass with her pups, although she made sure the two male wolves didn't get in on the feeding—more proof that alpha females are the bosses of wolf families.

On October 20, 2010, I saw all the Lamar wolves near my cabin at Silver Gate, Montana. They did a lot of howling. When 06 was close to the road, two cars stopped and the passengers took pictures of her. She ignored them. That was a bad sign. Wild wolves have a natural wariness of people, and 06 seemed to be losing that. I wasn't worried that she would ever harm a person. Wolf attacks on humans are extremely rare. The issue was legal hunting of wolves in nearby locations. If 06 did not regain that wariness, she could be an easy target for a hunter. ★ RICK

In November, 06 was chasing an elk cow several times her size. She eventually brought the elk down, but this time she had help from two of the pups who were old enough to participate in the hunts. 06 had been teaching the pups one of the most important lessons they needed to learn to survive. And her efforts were clearly working. When the lifeless elk cow lay on the ground, 06 stepped back and looked at her two young assistants, seemingly pleased that her offspring were turning those lessons into real-life action.

As winter dragged on, the snow became deeper and deeper, making travel more difficult for the elk, which were the main source of food for the Yellowstone wolves. But the deep snow presented something of a challenge for the wolves as well. Typically, when the wolves were on the move, one would lead, taking on the difficult job of breaking a trail through the snow for the others to follow. On one wintry day, 755 was leading the Lamar wolves, with 754 and 06 behind him. The pups, however, were following a different route and having trouble. The adults had gotten quite a distance ahead when 754, always aware of the pups, stopped and waited for them to catch up. The younger wolves then found the path that had been created by the adults and were able to make much better progress.

When the pups caught up with the adults, one of the young wolves got into a chasing game with its mother. 06 chased the pup and pinned it, playfully nipping as the pup pawed at her. Then the pup leaped up and took off. When it outran its mother, it turned around and came back so the game could continue. Again she pinned the pup, and then got into a similar game with another pup. The deep snow had brought out the playful side of the pack, with both adults and pups getting in on the fun.

In December the Lamar wolves were back at Slough Creek. On a nearby ridge, nine members of the neighboring Agate pack had gathered. The two packs were howling back and forth. 472, the Agate alpha female, was 06's mother, and they likely recognized the sound the other was making.

Though 472 had been born to Wolf 40, a horrible tyrant of a female, she was raised by Wolf 42, 40's sister. 42 was the exact opposite of 40, and was both a kind and capable leader who became the lifelong mate of one of Yellowstone's most famous males, Wolf 21. Wolf 42 ended up raising 40's pups after the nasty sister was mortally wounded by 42 and some of the younger Druid females to keep 40 from killing 42's newborn pups.

472 died not long after this encounter. The Agate pack had a high number of offspring move on to lead their own packs, and 472's daughter—the remarkable 06—was one of the best examples of this trend. Clearly, 472 and other Agate alphas were devoted parents who passed on many of the leadership qualities that had made them great leaders in their own time.

In mid-December, Wolf 586, the Agate pack's old alpha male, was howling from the area around Specimen

Ridge. The Lamar wolves responded with a group howl. Perhaps because he was old and his hearing wasn't as good as it once was, 586 apparently thought the howls he was hearing were from his own family and started moving toward them.

As the Lamars came out of the trees, 586 saw them but continued to move forward, still mistaking them for his own family. Finally realizing his error, he turned and ran. The Lamars easily caught and pinned him. At first he tried being submissive, but then changed his strategy and fought them. Despite his age and being outnumbered seven to one, he was doing a good job of defending himself. Again he ran, but realizing he couldn't outrun the Lamars, he turned, faced them, and fought. The old wolf alternated between running for his life, taking several bites on the hind end while he fled, and stopping to face his attackers. Finally, as 586 was once again running, and getting close to the river, 755 stopped. The other Lamars followed his example and let the old Agate alpha run to safety.

That behavior had been seen before in other wolves. Years earlier, Wolf 8 and Wolf 21 had avoided killing defeated rivals. Now, a few generations later, the Lamar pack was behaving the same way. An old wolf that could do them no real harm had been allowed to return to his home pack and territory.

◇ ◇ ◇

As the year 2011 got underway, there were seven wolves in the Lamar pack, eight in the neighboring Agates, and fifteen in the Blacktail pack that had been started by Wolf 302. That pack was located farther to the west of the Agates.

One of the jobs of the people who study the Yellowstone wolves is to put tracking collars on a few members of each pack. In order to safely do this job, a tranquilizer dart is shot at a wolf from a helicopter. It puts the wolf to sleep long enough for the park employees to fit the animal with a collar and give it a number.

The Yellowstone wolf biologists use a helicopter to capture park wolves so that they can be radio-collared for research purposes. Collaring takes place in the winter so the deep snow will slow the wolves as they run from the helicopter. In some cases, a net is fired from the copter to capture the wolf. In other situations, biologists fire a special gun that hits a wolf with a tranquilizer dart. Once a wolf is down, the biologists check for health issues and draw blood for DNA analysis. Then a specialized collar is placed around the wolf's neck. The collars broadcast a signal that allows researchers to find the wolves and study what they are doing. If the wolf later dies, the collar gives off a special "mortality signal," triggered after twelve hours of no activity, and the researchers will hike out to the site to determine the cause of death. About a third of the wolves in Yellowstone have radio collars. ★ RICK

The wolf project tries to have at least two wolves in each pack collared so park staff can keep track of their whereabouts. When the project biologists collar the wolves, they also weigh them, check their health, and take genetic samples so their ancestry can be charted. Each collared wolf is assigned a number for record keeping. Uncollared wolves are not numbered. Instead, they are referred to either by an easily identifiable physical feature (remember Triangle?) or some biographical aspect that sets them apart from other wolves—like the 06 Female, whose name comes from the year of her birth.

In mid-January, the Lamar and Agate wolves howled at each other from opposite sides of the valley. Eventually, both packs moved off, away from each other. Not long after that, though, an Agate pup got separated from his pack and came dangerously close to the Lamars. The pup howled and the Lamars howled back, but there was no attempt to cause any harm to the wayward pup. These incidents, combined with the earlier encounter when the Lamars had spared the life of the old Agate alpha, Wolf 586, seemed to indicate that the two packs were willing to coexist without the kind of fighting and nastiness that existed between some packs.

Perhaps of more importance was the fact that the Agates' territory was between the Lamar pack and the Mollie's, a much nastier pack that often leaned toward violence to achieve their goals. The Mollie's had previously resided in Lamar Valley, and if they decided they wanted to reclaim their former territory, things could turn ugly.

With mating season underway and denning time not far off, 06 chose a new location for her den, one she felt was even better than her choice of the previous year. It was an important decision. 06 knew that, and chose the place she felt would afford this year's litter of pups the best and safest shelter to meet the world: the Druid den forest. The location she chose was, in fact, the same den where Wolf 40 had once had a litter that included Wolf 472, 06's mother.

Now, eleven years later, 06 would be having her pups in the same den that her grandmother had given birth to her mother.

The pups' father was again 755, though 754 had tried, unsuccessfully, to be part of the breeding program as well. 755 ensured that didn't happen. Instead, 754 continued in his role as guardian, playmate, and uncle to the previous year's pups, now yearlings.

In mid-March, 06 was halfway through her two-month pregnancy. She spent a fair amount of time off by herself, preparing the den for the arrival of the pups. It had been a long, cold, difficult winter for the prey animals, and when 06 came across a large elk calf that was in poor health, she immediately attacked, despite being well into her pregnancy. The calf tried to fight her off but ultimately failed. For 06, the hunt had been a success, but it had also taken a toll. She was so exhausted from the effort that she walked off and bedded down for a while. Finally, after a forty-five-minute nap, she went back to the calf carcass and fed.

It was around that time that park staff received news of a condition in elk called chronic wasting disease (CWD). It is a debilitating sickness found in deer and elk, and is often spread from sick animals to healthy ones—it can also infect the meat consumed by humans. Wolves are not affected by CWD and, in fact, by eliminating animals with CWD, they help to prevent the spread of the disease. The elk calf that 06 took down that spring had stumbled as it tried to move away from her. That stumble may have been an indication that the elk had CWD. If that was the case, 06, in addition to accessing the nourishment she would need when the pups were born, had eliminated a carrier of the dreaded disease. ★ RICK

As 06's due date neared, she joined the males and the yearling pups at a carcass not far from where she was denning. Normally, 06 was dominant at a feeding, but this time was different. She lowered her head and acted like a newborn pup or a low-ranking adult. Even though there was a carcass at hand, she went to 755 and licked his face to get him to regurgitate a feeding for her. This uncharacteristic behavior was likely carefully planned.

It seemed as if 06 was looking ahead. She knew she would need the family to bring her food in that way while she was with the newborn pups, and so she was training her packmates—showing them what she would need them to do in just a short time.

Early April brought warm temperatures and huge amounts of snow that made it difficult for the wolves to travel. Soon 06 went into her den and stayed there for ten days. She had given birth and was with her pups almost constantly during their first days of life. In the early days of a pup's life, they cannot control their own body heat and have to keep warm by snuggling up to their mother. 06 stayed with her pups in order to keep them warm and well fed from nursing.

After a week or so, when she emerged from the den, 06 had regained enough strength to pursue a group of bighorn rams. Clearly, giving birth to her second litter hadn't slowed her down.

In fact, just a few days later 06 was hunting again, this time with 755 and a male yearling from 06's previous litter, who had been given the name Dark Gray. The young male found the carcass of an elk calf, picked it up, and carried it off. Eventually he set the calf on the ground and walked away. When 755 moved toward the carcass, Dark Gray came back quickly, growled at the alpha male, and began to feed. 755 settled a little way off and watched his son eat its fill. When the young wolf left the carcass, this time for good, 755 picked away at what was left. The episode was an example of what seemed like an unwritten rule in wolf packs—sort of like finders keepers, where "ownership rights" are respected by both male and female wolves regardless of where the finder happened to be in the hierarchy of the pack.

Soon after that, the Lamars brought down a bull elk. 755 tore off a leg and headed to the den to feed 06 and her pups, who were just beginning to eat meat. Showing his dedication to the role of provider for his family, 755 would regurgitate meat for both the mother and the pups, and leave the leg as well.

June brought its warmth to Yellowstone, and 06 emerged from the den with five healthy, active pups in tow—three blacks and two grays. She watched as her pups romped and wrestled and nipped playfully at one another. She seemed proud of her family but was ever watchful for the dangers that could occur at any moment. She knew from her experience with her first litter that there were potential threats—lots of them and not far off—and she was ready to face whatever trouble might come along.

A few days later, the seven adult members of the Lamar pack brought down a cow elk near Slough Creek. The creek had flooded that spring and was still high as spring rolled into summer. After feeding for a while, 06 left the kill with an elk leg in her mouth. She swam through some of the flooded area, holding the elk leg out of the water. When she came to a strip of land that sat between two channels of water, she dug a hole and buried the elk leg.

A half hour later, however, one of the yearlings arrived at the site, dug up the leg, and carried it off. Of course, 06 had done the very same thing to 754 a few times. Now one of her offspring had learned the trick and used it on her mother. Apparently, the "respecting ownership" principle did not apply to buried meat!

In wolf families, as in human families, offspring learn a lot from their parents. But sometimes the learning happens the other way as well, with parents learning from their young. Earlier that summer, female yearling 776 came to a bridge that was spanning a fast-moving stream called Soda Butte Creek. After first sniffing the bridge and then taking a few steps onto it before retreating, 776 got into a crouch and crossed the structure—an unusual action for wolves, who would normally prefer to swim across a body of water. For a wolf it is usually a good idea to be wary of new things, for they might be harmful. It's a trait that might save a wolf from stepping into a trap.

A week later, though, 06 crossed the same bridge, this time with Dark Gray following her. Had she been following her daughter's example? It seems quite likely. Even more impressive, after 06 crossed the bridge, she came to a road, stopped, and looked both ways before crossing. Not only had she mastered a bridge-crossing, but she also seemed to understand the concept of two-way traffic.

◇ ◇ ◇

The care and feeding of a group of pups can be physically taxing, but 06 seldom showed signs of being less than equal to the task. By August her pups needed more nourishment to feed their growing bodies. That month, 06 was feeding on a fresh carcass 6 miles (almost 10 kilometers) from the den. On a hot summer morning, 06 made the trek to the carcass, fed on it, and then returned to the den to regurgitate a feeding for the pups. She made the round trip three times that day, twice in the morning and once in the evening, traveling a total of 36 miles (58 kilometers). Her incredible strength and stamina provided further evidence that she was part of a small group of truly remarkable females who had lived in and roamed Yellowstone National Park in the seventeen years since the Wolf Reintroduction Project began.

During that same month, the yearling called Dark Gray was often away from the rest of the Lamars, an indication that he was getting ready to find a mate and start a pack of his own. But the remaining three yearlings and three adults were all actively involved in raising this year's litter. 06 would sometimes bed down nearby and watch the yearlings and adult males 755 and 754 chasing and wrestling with the pups, two of the pups' favorite forms of play. They were a tight-knit family—but they would soon face a difficult and very dangerous test.

Early on August 30, I spotted the Lamar wolves south of the road that went through the valley, up the Lamar River. All five pups were traveling with the adults. Two people on horseback saw the wolves and rode toward them. All the wolves, including the pups, seemed afraid of the horses and the people, and ran away. In contrast, later that day the pups and adults chased a grizzly. The bear soon stopped, and the pups casually walked around it. The pups had already learned how to handle themselves around grizzlies and did not seem afraid of them. But the horses were something new, and their instinct was to avoid them. That was a good thing, since most of the hunting parties outside the park used horses. ★ RICK

6

Danger and More Danger

The Mollie's wolf pack had a long-standing grudge with the Druids, dating back to 1996 when the Druids had attacked the ancestors of the current Mollie's in Lamar Valley, killing the alpha male and all the newborn pups. Wolves in the Agate, Blacktail, and Lamar packs were descendants of those Druids and were likely viewed as enemies by the Mollie's, who had a reputation for violence and had returned a few times to Lamar Valley in recent years. The reappearances left the Yellowstone wolf researchers wondering if the Mollie's intended to reclaim the territory of their ancestors. During one of those intrusions, the Mollie's killed the famed Druid alpha female Wolf 42.

Wolves lead lives that are full of challenges. Of all the female wolves I have known, the one who had to endure the most adversity was Wolf 42. Two years in a row her ill-tempered and violent sister, Wolf 40, killed 42's

newborn pups. When it was about to happen a third time, 42 stood up to her sister and was joined by some of the younger Druid females who could no longer tolerate 40's aggression. And though she had every reason to want further revenge against her sister, 42 showed a much gentler, kinder side. When 40 died of the wounds she suffered in the fight with the Druid females, 42 raised 40's orphan pups with her own, a huge task. 42 then took over 40's role as the alpha female and immediately displayed a different kind of leadership based on cooperation. Her devotion to her mate, the legendary Wolf 21, to her pups, and to her pack made her one of the greatest of the Yellowstone female wolves and one of the most loved by all of us involved with the Wolf Reintroduction Project. In the small town of Gardiner, just outside the north entrance to Yellowstone, there is a visitors center and store. Among the exhibits on display is a statue of 42. It is fitting that this amazing female wolf is the one who is honored with a statue. She is one of the feature wolves in Book 2 of this series: *A Time of Legends*. ★ RICK

Changes in the Mollie's hierarchy were about to take the pack's violent tendencies to another level. In September, the Mollie's alpha male, Wolf 495, was killed during an encounter with a bison. That meant that the alpha female, Wolf 486, was related to all of the remaining males in the pack. Because wolves do not mate with relatives, 486 left the Mollie's to find an unrelated male from another pack.

Stepping into the vacancy at the top of the pack was 486's three-year-old daughter, Wolf 686, a particularly nasty and aggressive female. Just five days after she took over as alpha female, the alpha male of the Mary Mountain pack, a group that lived in the central part of the park, was attacked and killed by the Mollie's. This act of violence against a neighboring pack was a sign of what was to come.

In December of that year, the Mollie's numbered nineteen. And they continued to move closer to the Lamars. During that time, the Agate alpha male was killed in another wolf attack—and the Mollie's were once again the prime suspects. The Agates lived in an area between the Lamars and the Mollie's, and the killing of their alpha male suggested that the Mollie's were intent on moving closer to Lamar Valley—and to the Lamar pack, which numbered only eleven wolves: three adults, three yearlings and five pups.

By mid-December the two packs were howling back and forth at one another, the Lamars on the south side of Lamar Valley and the Mollie's on the north. It was looking more and more like a battle was inevitable, and if and when it happened, the outnumbered Lamars would have a tough time holding their own.

The day after the howl, the Lamars traveled well to the east, an indication that they were aware of the Mollie's overwhelming numbers and were not eager to risk a fight. But the Mollie's kept coming. Soon enough, they were at Slough Creek, just a few miles away.

Adding to the danger was the Mollie's knowledge about the Druid den forest. They had spent plenty of time in the area and knew exactly where it was. If 06 was to use that area for denning again—and denning season was only a few months off—there was a good chance the Mollie's could invade the area and attack 06 and her litter of helpless newborn pups.

On January 1, the Mollie's were feeding on a fresh elk kill at Slough Creek; the following day they were still there and howling. The Lamars, 8 miles (about 13 kilometers) away, howled back. At one point the Mollie's set off following a scent trail, hoping to get to the Lamars, but they became confused by other scent trails and followed one that actually led away from the Lamars. For now, 06 had given them the slip.

A few days later, three Blacktail wolves, the alpha pair and an adult male called Medium Gray, were following one of the Mollie's scent trails and howling. Minutes later, nine members of the Mollie's, who had heard those howls, attacked. The three Blacktails fled, with Medium Gray going one way and the two alphas going another. The Mollie's chased Medium Gray, and it wasn't long before they caught and savagely killed him—yet another victim of the pack's seemingly relentless attacks. In a span of five months they had killed five rival wolves: three members of the Agate pack, Medium Gray from the Blacktails, and the Mary Mountain alpha male.

The Blacktails had made a drastic mistake in getting too close to the Mollie's, and Medium Gray paid dearly for that mistake. As for the nearby Lamars, 06 was being much more careful, and so far had been able to avoid contact with the dangerous enemy pack.

In late January the Mollie's were on the move again, this time heading south to their home territory in Pelican Valley, where they had long supported themselves by hunting bison. But before they left the northern section of the park, they killed two more members of the Agate pack. What was worrisome about these killings was that the victims were former Mollie's. If the Mollie's were willing to turn on former members of their own pack, it seemed as if their violence had no boundaries—and that it was just a matter of time until they went after 06 and the Lamars.

◇ ◇ ◇

Unfortunately for 06, the Mollie's weren't the only danger to guard against. During one of the darting and collaring operations, 06 and one of her yearling pups were captured. After they'd been collared, they were flown by helicopter to the north side of the valley, which would be safer as there were no Mollie's in that part of the park at that time. They were taken from the helicopter and laid gently on the forest floor. While they were sleeping off the effects of the tranquilizing drugs, three members of the wolf project staff—Colby Anton, Julie Tasch, and Rebecca Raymond—stayed close by to make sure nothing happened to the two wolves, who were in a completely defenseless state.

As 06 and the pup that had been given the number 820 slept on, a herd of seventy-five bison were on the move—and headed directly for the two helpless wolves. The bison had caught the scent of the wolves and continued toward them. If they got to the incapacitated 06 and her pup, it was likely the bison would trample them to death.

The wolf project team members had to do something, and they didn't have much time. There were two large boulders about 75 yards (almost 69 meters) from where the wolves lay, still completely asleep. The boulders weren't the perfect solution, but they were the team's only hope.

They picked up 06 and ran through knee-deep snow to get to the boulders. Then they did the same thing with the pup. The two wolves were now next to the boulders, not completely out of sight but with at least a little protection from the oncoming bison.

When the bison reached the site, they slowed down, curious as to what was going on. They couldn't see the wolves, but they *could* see three people who smelled like wolves, thanks to their handling of the sleeping animals. As the bison got closer and closer to the boulders, the researchers ran toward the herd, yelling and waving their trekking poles, spraying bear repellent, and even throwing snow at the huge animals.

For a couple of minutes no one was sure what was going to happen next. If the bison charged, the still-unconscious wolves and their human protectors would be in grave danger.

Then, for no apparent reason, the bison seemed to lose interest. They continued their forward march, but they passed by the wolves and the researchers without causing any harm. The three team members' courage and desire to protect the wolves at all costs had won the day. A few hours later, 06 and 820 were awake and alert and back with the pack, completely unaware of the danger they had so narrowly escaped.

7

Standoff in Lamar Valley

February 9 saw the first serious skirmish between the Mollie's and the Lamars. All eleven members of the Lamar pack were near Slough Creek, and ten members of the Mollie's—minus 686, the unpleasant female—weren't far away. The Lamars howled and, in response, the Mollie's charged. Despite the relatively even numbers, the Lamars used a clever tactic typically used when one group is outnumbered by another—they scattered in every direction.

The Mollie's were able to catch one black pup and pin it. They attacked the pup for about a minute, until they were distracted by other Lamars running nearby. The pup, though injured, was able to get up and run away. The Mollie's followed the pup's scent trail but were unable to find it. That night, 06 made the smart decision to move the pack 23 miles (about 37 kilometers) to the east in order to put as much distance as possible between her pack and the marauding Mollie's.

A few days later the Lamars were on the move near their home den, with the injured black pup at the back of the group, clearly hurting but determined to keep up with the rest of the pack. The Mollie's returned to their home territory in the Pelican Valley, and for a while peace reigned over Lamar Valley. The Mollie's had a problem of their own, however, as the nasty alpha female, 686, had not been able to recruit a male to join the pack. That was necessary, as she was related to all of the males in the Mollie's, but so far she'd had no luck finding a willing candidate.

Thinking about 686's situation, I often wondered how she would ever find a male willing to risk pairing off with such a violent female. What would she do to a mate who displeased her? ★ RICK

The February breeding season arrived in Yellowstone, and 06 mated several times with 755, which meant that she would likely be having her third litter around April 20. It was a tough time for 754. His brother kept him away from 06 during the breeding season, so he tried to get Middle Gray interested in him instead. Unfortunately, she was having none of it, and since male wolves eventually accept rejection and do not try to force themselves on females who don't want them, 754 was unable to mate.

In early March, Wolf 06 and the other Lamars were back at the Druid den forest, her preferred denning area. One chilly spring day saw 06 and 755 playfully romping around. Wolves love playing with each other, so this wasn't unusual behavior, but it was also, once again, a strategic move on the part of 06. She knew those playtimes would strengthen the bond between her and 755, which would allow her to count on the alpha male to support her and her pups when they were born. As her due date drew closer, 06 also spent a lot of time around the den, cleaning it out and ensuring that no rival wolves had been anywhere near it.

Even though her focus was on the den, 06 had to keep tabs on the Mollie's. And it wasn't long before the rival pack was once again nearby. This time, though, 06 and the other Lamars did not do any howling; it would have given away their position. When the Mollie's were far in the distance, the Lamars exchanged howls with the Agates, a smaller pack they were on reasonably friendly terms with, and a pack that, like the Lamars, had plenty of trouble with the Mollie's.

The Mollie's continued to come and go from Lamar Valley, far from their home territory in Pelican Valley. Most of the Yellowstone wolf packs are elk hunters. But the Mollie's and their original alpha female, Wolf 5, had been driven out of Lamar Valley back in 1996 by the original Druids, led by the cruel female Wolf 40. In the years that followed, the Mollie's had perfected the difficult task of taking down the massive bison that were prevalent in the Pelican Valley region of the park.

At the end of March, the Mollie's alpha female, 686, and other pack members had gone back to their home denning area. If 686 was pregnant, 06 and the Lamars would at least be safe from any Mollie's attacks during the denning season.

That spring, the Lamars numbered ten. Two of the young males had left the pack in search of mates, leaving the three founding adults, 06, 755, and 754, along with two young female adults, 776 and Middle Gray, and the five pups from the previous year, now yearlings. One of the black yearlings soon disappeared, bringing the number of Lamars down to nine.

On April 1, the short-lived time of peace came to an abrupt end. While 06 was away from her den, she was spotted by a group of fifteen Mollie's. The chase was on, with the pregnant 06 racing as fast as she could along the road that ran through that part of the park. The Mollie's weren't far back, and they were closing ground. But as some vehicles came down the road, the Mollie's, who hadn't encountered many vehicles in their more remote home area, gave up the chase.

06 was savvy enough about roads and cars and trucks to use them to her advantage and escape the marauders for the moment. Soon, 754 was there to

calmly lead 06 and the rest of the Lamars back to the den. The reappearance of the Mollie's in Lamar territory made one thing clear: 686 had not found a mate and had not had a litter of pups—and that was not good news.

It wasn't just the Lamars the Mollie's were at war with. The northern wolf packs that included the Agates and the Blacktails were also in danger. On April 11, the Agate alpha female, Wolf 471, was killed by the Mollie's. She was carrying seven fetuses at the time of her death, and her loss was devastating for the Agates.

As 06's due date of April 20 rolled around, the first flowers had begun to bloom. It was the perfect time for the birth of a new litter of wolf pups. A couple of days later, most of the Lamar family was gathered around a bull elk they had taken down not far from the denning site. 06 briefly emerged from the den to feed, and then hurried back to her newborn pups, who needed the warmth of their mother to survive the still-chilly spring days and nights.

On April 25, sixteen Mollie's were gathered near Slough Creek. None of the females looked pregnant, which meant the lure of their home base territory was not particularly strong. It had only been a few weeks since the pack had killed Agate alpha female 471—one of seven wolves the Mollie's had killed in recent months—and it now looked as if 06 and the Lamars were next on their hit list. Soon the Mollie's were working their way east, heading directly for 06's den.

All at once, there was an explosion of wolves from out of the forest. In the lead was 06, running for her life with sixteen Mollie's in pursuit. She'd had her pups only a few days before, and could not run fast. But she was leading the deadly Mollie's away from the den where her helpless pups lay waiting for their mother's return.

As the Mollie's closed in on her, that return was very much in doubt. To make matters worse, 06 had chosen a path that led to the top of a cliff. When she reached the cliff's edge, she would have no choice but to turn and fight. And it wasn't likely to end well. As good and as brave a fighter as 06 was, she would have no chance against an enemy force the size of the Mollie's.

But 06 had a plan—a very dangerous plan. Instead of stopping at the cliff's edge, she went right over—and raced almost straight down a steep gully strewn with sharp-edged loose rocks. The rocks cut into the pads on her paws, but she didn't slow down.

She reached the bottom and crossed the road, pausing just long enough to glance back at the cliff to see if her pursuers had risked making the same descent she had. They had not. The Mollie's milled around for a few seconds, wondering how 06 had been able to escape and thinking about what to do next. They spotted another Lamar female, Middle Gray, one of 06's two-year-old daughters from her very first litter. The Mollie's raced off after her. But Middle Gray was the fastest of all the Lamar wolf family, and she soon left the Mollie's far behind.

06 wasn't out of danger yet. The brave mother had joined up with the yearling 820, and together they had run to the top of a slope. The two of them looked down from that lofty perch toward the den. There was a problem, a serious problem: The Mollie's were in the forest between 06 and the den. She and Middle Gray had done all they could to lure the Mollie's away from the den and the pups tucked inside. Now it was up to 754 and 755. What would the two brothers do? What *could* they do?

They would either stand their ground against impossible odds or they would run away and abandon the pups to be killed by the Mollie's. A couple of years earlier, the two Lamar males had faced a similar situation when a huge grizzly bear had approached the den. The brothers' strategy was for 755 to charge at the bear while 754 stood guard at the entrance to the den.

They employed a similar strategy on this day, standing shoulder to shoulder to block the entrance to the den. 755 and 754 were willing to fight to the death to protect the helpless week-old pups.

The Mollie's were big wolves, most of them bigger than the majority of the Lamars. The exception was 754, who was the biggest of the Lamars. He faced the

Mollie's, standing tall, fearless, and ready. 755 was closer to the Mollie's, his growl and bared teeth a challenge to the invaders.

The Mollie's weighed their options. The price they would have to pay in this fight, even though they would likely win it in the end, was too great. They slowly turned and left the Druid den forest. The Lamars, adults and pups, were safe.

The next morning, the Mollie's were far away to the west hunting bison. They stopped and howled. The Lamars defiantly howled back, knowing that they had stood up to the bully wolf pack and won.

Despite their unsuccessful attempt to get to the Lamar family den, the Mollie's did not leave the area. The first day of May brought sunnier skies to Yellowstone, and the Mollie's continued to bring dark clouds to the area. That day, the body of Wolf 838, also known as Big Blaze, lay in a meadow near Antelope Creek. Once the Agate alpha male, he had eventually joined the Blacktail pack. And he was now the eighth victim of the Mollie's seemingly endless violence. Big Blaze had been born into the Druid pack.

Wolf 686, the alpha female of the Mollie's, had still not found a male to mate with. However, some of the younger Mollie's females had gotten together with some males from outside of the Mollie's, and it looked like they were forming a new pack. A big gray appeared to be the alpha female, and a former Blacktail male known as Puff seemed to have assumed the alpha male role. That new group became known as the Junction Butte pack, and they later used the den at Slough Creek to have their pups.

The wolf researchers watched the den forest every day hoping to catch a glimpse of 06's new pups. Finally, four healthy pups—two blacks and two grays—walked into an opening in the trees. They were the pups who had been saved by the heroism of brothers 755 and 754.

After the wolf family left the den later that spring, the wolf researchers hiked up into the forest to examine the den. The vast majority of wolf dens are burrows dug into the ground. But 06 found a cave-like enclave under a huge house-sized boulder and had her pups there. The back end of the cave was only a few inches high. That meant if 754 and 755 had died defending the den, the little pups could have squeezed into that area and been beyond the reach of the enemy pack. The discovery of that den site was yet another example of 06's extraordinary intelligence.

★ RICK

06 and 755 were the alphas of the Lamar pack, but 754 was a lot more than a favorite uncle to the pack's pups. He was the biggest and strongest of the Lamars and had displayed his courage during the standoff with the Mollie's. He was also valuable on hunts. He showed just how valuable he could be on a hot mid-July day when the Lamars had chased a big bull elk into the

Lamar River. An experienced elk will often take to deep water, knowing that his long legs allow him to stand while the wolves have to swim to get at him, which puts them at a distinct disadvantage.

On this particular day, 06 and 755 slipped into the river and began to dog-paddle against the strong current to get at the elk. When they got close, he ran downstream past them. The two alphas now had to turn and swim after him and, once again, as they closed in, the wily elk ran past them, this time upstream.

Finally the elk was in shallow water. 06 leaped for his throat but the elk dodged away. At the same time, 755 tried to grab a leg, but he too missed. While all this was going on, 754 and the other Lamar wolves stayed on the shore and watched the alphas struggle with the elk.

Then, 755 decided to try a new strategy. He got out of the water, trotted upstream from the bull, and then floated down toward him. The massive elk turned to face the oncoming 755, reared up, and tried to strike the wolf on the head and back with his front hooves. 755 was able to dodge the blow and got in a bite at the elk's shoulder. The elk shook him off. The two alpha wolves were exhausted from the effort. 06 got out of the water a few times to roll in the grass and shake the cold water out of her fur. Then she'd get back in the water for another try. Finally the two alphas climbed out of the river to rest.

They waited a long time before getting back in the water. This time they finally had some success. 755 got hold of one of the bull's legs while 06 bit into his side. Sensing an opportunity, 06 then tried to bite the neck of the tiring animal. She was able to hold on to the elk, and together 06 and 755 dragged the elk down into the water. It was at that critical moment 06 lost her grip on the elk—the huge animal was about to break free.

754 swung into action, jumping into the water. He swam straight to the elk and leaped up to deliver a killing bite to its throat. Three of the younger Lamar adult wolves followed 754 into the water to join in the fight. The two alphas and 754 were finally able to pull the elk's head lower and lower, until its nose was under water and it drowned.

The pack then dragged the elk carcass onto shore and fed for some time, with 06 consuming a large portion so she could regurgitate it for her four pups when she was back in the den. The fight with the elk had lasted almost an hour and a half, and it was persistence and teamwork—notably the quick thinking and tremendous strength of 754, working alongside the pack's alphas—that ultimately led to success.

◇ ◇ ◇

A few weeks later, in early August, the main group of Mollie's were once again in their home territory in

Pelican Valley. At the same time, former Blacktail males 777 and Puff had formed the new Junction Butte pack with four young Mollie's females. One of those females was Wolf 822, who had been part of the group that had tried to mount the attack on 06's den in late April.

The four pups in 06's third litter were busying themselves trying different techniques to trap some of the grasshoppers that were in abundance that year. They alternated between snapping at the insects as they jumped around and pouncing on them when the grasshoppers were stationary.

On August 3, Wolf 777 and the newly formed pack were feeding on an old bison carcass a few miles from the Lamars' den. Eight of the nine Lamar adults, with 06 in the lead, were headed directly toward them, tails raised to indicate they were planning to attack.

The group at the carcass saw the Lamars coming and ran off to the west, with 06 and company in hot pursuit. 06 sniffed the scent trail of the trespassers and identified Wolf 822. When 822 split off from the rest of the fleeing group and ran north, the Lamars left the main group and went after her. The former Mollie's female raced toward the park road, and then veered east into a series of rolling hills. 06 continued the chase, with the rest of the Lamars right behind her. 755 left the group and took a shortcut that would take him to a point that would meet up with 822. Soon enough, 755 was right behind 822—and gaining fast.

He lunged forward, caught 822, and pulled her down. The other Lamars quickly arrived on the scene and joined the attack.

The other wolves in 822's group howled, and all of the Lamars—except for 06—took off after them. Her anger was evident as she bit at her adversary again and again, viciously shaking her head back and forth to inflict maximum damage. Finally, 06 backed off. Her grandfather was the famous Wolf 21, who had never killed a defeated opponent. But her grandmother was the notorious Wolf 40, who had made a habit of bullying the other females in her pack and killing her sister's newborn pups.

During the attack, 06 seemed to be channeling her grandmother. But when she heard more howls from the other group of wolves, she delivered one final bite before leaving the injured 822 and moving off. Despite the ferocity of her attack, 06 stopped short of giving a fatal bite to the throat that would have ended 822's life. In that regard, she seemed to reflect some of her grandfather's temperament.

06, her fury having subsided, picked up a stick and headed back toward the den. She had gone from fierce avenger to devoted mother, taking a toy back to her offspring. 06 was clearly adept at both roles.

A few hours later, 822 died from her wounds. She was the latest victim in a feud that had begun almost a decade earlier. The hostilities each of those family lines felt for the other had not eased through the years, and it didn't look like they would go away anytime soon.

In fact, it wasn't long before the Mollie's struck again. This time the victim was Wolf 777, the male who, along with Puff, had started the new pack with some of the Mollie's females. That death brought the total number of wolves that had been killed by the Mollie's to nine. Why would the vicious alpha female 686 lead the Mollie's in an attack on 777? Was it solely because he too was a descendant of those early Druids and had fallen victim to her seemingly insatiable appetite for revenge? Or maybe it was jealousy. 686 was still unable to attract a mate and have pups. Perhaps she was enraged that some of the other females in the family had been able to do those things. Or was she so controlling that the decision made by some family members to split off from the main pack and strike out on their own incensed her? All were possibilities.

There was calm after the killing of Wolf 777, as the Mollie's finally returned to their home territory. They had spent eight months in and around the area that was home to the Lamars, the Agates, and the Blacktails.

Despite all the time that the Mollie's had been in Lamar territory—and despite their superior numbers and bloodthirsty leader—not a single member of 06's pack, adult or pup, had been lost. It was a testament to the alpha female's courage, intelligence, and leadership skills.

The new group established by 777 and Puff and the young Mollie's females became well established in the Slough Creek region. Because a previous pack in the area had been called the Slough Creek pack, the new group was given the name Junction Butte pack, after a nearby landmark, and Puff became their alpha male (he was later radio-collared and became known as Wolf 911). An uncollared Mollie's gray became the alpha female. The merging of wolves from these two feuding families created what became a successful, long-lasting pack that continues to this day.

★ RICK

8

Good Times and Bad Times

With the threat from the Mollie's finally gone, at least for the time being, the Lamar pack members were able to relax, hunt, and play in the summer sun. One pleasant August day found all of them feeding on a bison carcass. 754 was like an energetic yearling as he played with the pups. First, he joined in a chasing game with one of the females; then he cavorted with Middle Gray. 755 was bedded down nearby but didn't get involved with the play session.

The next morning there was more play, but this time it was led by 06, who apparently did not want to miss out on the fun. She seemed carefree now that the Mollie's were gone. She nipped at a yearling, romped off, then returned and nipped the yearling again. These were good times for the Lamars, and they were making the most of it.

A few days later, most of the adult Lamars had crossed the road to feed on another bison carcass. But

754 stayed back with the pups, passing up a meal in order to watch over them. He continued to be the favorite uncle and protector of this set of pups, just as he had been with 06's first two litters.

Summer rolled on, and a few weeks later 06 and the rest of the Lamar adults left the den area and headed out to hunt. They came to the road and were getting ready to cross it when a large bus and several cars stopped to watch and nab pictures. The vehicles all parked at exactly the spot where 06 wanted to cross. Using a big red stop sign—like the ones used by school crossing guards—Rick and a law enforcement ranger managed to clear a section of the road of vehicles and stopped the oncoming traffic as well. Seeing the opening, 06, ever the leader, led the Lamars through it and they continued on their way.

In September, the fast-growing pups had followed the adults to an area south of that same road. It was the pups' first visit to the Norris rendezvous site—a place in which generations of Druid pups had spent countless hours. The pups sniffed around for a while, and then played together in what for them was a brand-new playground.

A week after the Lamars arrived at the Norris site, the adults took the four pups across the Lamar River to another popular rendezvous site called Chalcedony. The pups were soon racing around the meadow having fun. A year that had been filled with danger and the need to be ever watchful had finally evolved into a time of peace and, for the wolves of the Lamar pack, a time of fun and frivolity. The balance of power between the Mollies and the Lamars had shifted dramatically. The departure of several of the young Mollie's females to help form the Junction Butte pack, a group that was not aggressive toward the Lamars, meant that there were now only six Mollie's remaining, compared to thirteen wolves in the Lamar pack.

A few days later, the pups followed the adults out of the Chalcedony rendezvous site on a trek heading west. The alpha pair, 755 and 06, were especially playful during that journey. 755 chased 06. She easily outran him but then would race back toward him, forcing all of the other adults to jump out of the way or risk getting bowled over. 754 also had to jump to safety, but then he took off after her. 06 ran back to 755 and got him to chase her. Neither of the males could catch the fleet-footed 06. She was having fun, showing just how fast she really was.

Meanwhile, the younger adults were also playing among themselves. 06 came over, jumped into the group, and then took off and ran circles around the rest of the family.

A black pup came up with a new game. It found a plastic bottle, picked it up, and raced around the other pups, daring them to try to take the bottle. They took the dare, pursued the pup, and it dropped the bottle.

Another pup grabbed the bottle and took off. The game went on for a while, with first one wolf, then another—even 06 and 754—in possession of the bottle.

When they tired of that game, 755 and 06 started sparring, and then 754 joined in. It was an afternoon of wolf games. Eventually, 06 relaxed, lying down with her head on her paws. She looked over her family: the two males 755 and 754, the younger adults, and this year's pups. She had done an amazing job as a leader, a provider, and a teacher, and she could take pride in the results of her efforts. Unfortunately, it would be the last time the Lamars would enjoy a day like this.

Later that month the Lamars were in the Silver Gate area, not far from where Rick lives and also very close to the park boundary and the very dangerous legal wolf-hunting zone. Of course, the wolves had no way of knowing where the boundaries were or what the consequences could be if they continued to move back and forth across them.

Every fall, Native Americans John Potter (Ojibwe) and Scott Frazier (Santee and an enrolled Crow Tribal Member) come to the park to conduct a wolf blessing ceremony. They always invite people to join them. Their initial blessing took place in early 1995, when the first fourteen wolves from Alberta arrived in the park. During the 2012 ceremony, Scott made a profound statement about the success of the park's Wolf Reintroduction Project: "It is good to be part of putting something back rather than

taking something away," he said. That was a perfect way to describe the success of the project. John later added: "The original Canadian wolves that were brought in on the day Scott and I did our first blessing are gone now, but their spirits live on in the surrounding mountains." ★ RICK

In the second week of November the Lamar wolves left the park and unknowingly ended up in a section of Wyoming where the wolf-hunting season was ongoing. When the pack came back to Lamar Valley, one of their members—754—was missing. The Lamars had survived harsh western winters, they had fought off grizzly bears, and they had held their ground against one of the most deadly wolf packs to ever reside in Yellowstone. But there was no defense against humans with guns. And 754—the tough, fearless male who never got to be an alpha but was a huge contributor to the success of his pack and was loved by all of 06's pups—had been shot and killed 12 miles (about 19 kilometers) east of the park border.

The next day, a hunter stopped at the Wyoming game-check station and reported that he had shot a wolf. He said he had wanted to shoot the biggest wolf he could find, and 754 was the biggest wolf in the Lamar pack.

The following day, another Yellowstone wolf, 823, one of the young Mollie's females who had left that pack to form the Junction Butte pack, was also shot. She had ventured north of the park border into Montana. That area had no quota on the number of wolves that could be shot, and 823 was killed by a man who was working for a local hunting outfitter. His boss had told him not to shoot any collared wolves, but that didn't stop the man from shooting the collared 823. His boss fired him, and the outcry that followed that shooting resulted in a quota finally being imposed in that area to limit the number of wolves that could be killed.

Wolf 06 led the rest of the Lamars back to their forest den area. She stopped frequently to howl, and the others would join in as well. They were likely howling for 754. They didn't know he had been killed; they only knew that he was missing, so it made sense to head back to their home base and howl for him.

The Lamars continued to howl in the hopes that 754 would howl back. They picked away at a bison carcass that had been there a long time and had only scraps to offer. Several days later, on December 9, the Lamars were still howling as they returned to the area where they had last seen 754. They were searching for him and hoping that he would reappear.

But he would never howl again.

754 had been the seventh wolf hunted down and killed in that area with its quota of eight. That meant that only one more wolf could be shot in that hunting zone. Two days later, 06 was back in the area outside the park, very near where 754 had died. Still missing

her longtime partner and unwilling to give up the search for him, 06 had returned to look for him. She raised her head to howl to him but never got the chance. A shot rang out, and 06 fell. She became the eighth and final wolf to be shot as part of the quota for that area.

755 risked his life by attending to 06. He tried to get her up so they could get away from the hunters. He pawed at her and licked her wounds, but she remained motionless. 755 stayed with his mate for some time, only leaving when the hunter and his friend came to retrieve 06.

When the hunter took away 06's body, 755 and the other Lamars stayed nearby and continued to howl. They had to know that this would alert potential enemies to their position. But 755 ignored any danger to himself. He remained until he realized 06 was gone and they would never be together again.

The next morning I heard that the Junction Butte wolves were visible at Hellroaring Creek. I knew that a large crowd of wolf watchers would be gathered there. On my way I tried to plan out what I was going to say to all the people who were waiting to hear what we knew about the wolf that had been shot and were desperately hoping it wasn't 06. I got to the lot, saw some of the Junction Butte wolves, and turned to everyone and told them the news. Each person looked at me in stunned silence, then the emotions hit. One woman collapsed and started sobbing. I knelt down

and did what I could to comfort her. Then I went around to everyone else, and we shared stories of 06 and 754. That helped a bit. ★ RICK

06's family lingered in the area outside the park near where she and 754 had died, but they were not in danger from the hunters. 06's death had filled the quota, so no other wolves could be killed in that valley. In a sad sense, they were safe because of her.

A couple of days later the *New York Times* printed an obituary for 06. It read in part: "Yellowstone National Park's best-known wolf, beloved by many tourists and valued by scientists who tracked her movements, was shot and killed on Thursday outside the park's boundaries, Wyoming wildlife officials reported. The wolf... was the alpha female of the highly visible Lamar Canyon pack and had become so well known that some wildlife watchers referred to her as 'rock star.' The animal had been a tourist favorite for most of the past six years."

In 2014, the National Geographic Wild channel aired a documentary on 06 made by Montana filmmaker Bob Landis. It was titled *She Wolf*, and millions of people around the world watched it. Bob later interviewed me as an extra feature for the video release of the program. It was an honor to be able to share stories about 06 and tell millions of television viewers about my own experience with this amazing female. ★ RICK

9

Big Changes

The deaths of 06 and 754 meant that major changes were ahead for the Lamars. As 2013 got underway, 755 and daughters 776 and 820 were still in Lamar Valley, but the rest of the pack was outside the park. Regardless of location, a problem remained: 755 was closely related to all of the Lamar females and would not be able to breed with them.

He soon broke away from the rest of the Lamars and set out to look for a new mate. The Lamars outside the park were soon joined by a group of males from the disbanded Hoodoo pack. They formed a new pack and became a second edition of the Hoodoos.

Meanwhile, 755 searched several wolf territories hoping to find a mate. He finally met up with a gray Mollie's female, Wolf 759, in Lamar Valley. The attraction was immediate.

The Lamars quickly became aware of 755 and the female 759, and they wasted no time in making their feelings known. The long-standing feud between the Mollie's and the Lamars hadn't gone away—the pack clearly remembered the Mollie's attempt to raid 06's den. Once again revenge was on their minds. At their first opportunity they were able to separate 759 from 755 and took off after her. They finally caught and attacked her. She was eventually able to get back to 755, who had been howling for her, but she was bleeding and badly hurt. Unfortunately, she did not survive the attack. 759 had mated with 755 and was pregnant, so he lost not only her but also her unborn litter.

Once again 755 was without a mate. Though he had a brief connection with another gray female in the spring of 2013, she soon left the area, perhaps intimidated by neighboring packs. 755 would father no pups that year and would spend much of it as a lone, and lonely, wolf.

Following the confrontation with 759, the main group of Lamars left their home valley and denned in an area east of the park. Middle Gray stayed behind and was soon joined by her younger sister, the black Wolf 926. The two of them were based at the family's territory in Lamar Valley. Both were capable females, as would be expected of daughters of 06. But they would need a male partner to be able to produce wolf families in the future. And that's when fate stepped in: An uncollared male with an injured ear that stuck out at an odd angle ambled into Lamar Valley. A former member of the Hoodoo pack, he was looking for a mate or mates, and the two females needed a male. It was a perfect match, and the Lamar pack was reborn. That male was later collared and given the number 925.

By mid-April of that year, Middle Gray was getting ready to have pups. Meanwhile, 925 and 926 frequently left the den forest together to go on hunts or visit carcasses. They spent some time playing and scent-marking, the latter often a sign that they were the alpha pair. Yet 926 behaved in a clearly subordinate way toward her sister, which would indicate that Middle Gray was the alpha female.

By May, Middle Gray had given birth to two black pups. She was raising 06's grandbabies in the same den forest where 06's mother had been born in 2000. Shortly after the birth of the pups, 926 found the carcass of a bison that had died of natural causes. That carcass kept the family fed for a long time. When Middle Gray ventured out of the den, she licked the face of her sister, acknowledging that 926 was actually the alpha female in this little family.

In September, Wolf 686, the vicious alpha female of the Mollie's, was killed by other wolves. During her time as the Mollie's leader, the pack had killed at least nine wolves from other packs and mounted an unsuccessful attack on 06's den that would have resulted in the deaths of that year's Lamar pups were it not for the courage of 06 and the two males 755 and 754. Wolf 686 had never succeeded in raising surviving pups, and after several years of being unable to attract a mate, she eventually left the Mollie's and lived as a lone wolf until the time of her death. After being such an aggressive female and killing many other wolves, it was not surprising that she met a violent end.

And there were more changes among the Yellowstone wolves. Wolf 755 had met up with a female, Wolf 889, and she had become his new mate. The pair were on Specimen Ridge, high above Lamar Valley. It looked like at last, more than a year after losing 06, he had found a female that would be the kind of partner he needed. 889 was a capable hunter, and proved it one fall morning when the two of them were hunting. There were hundreds of elk in the area, but 889 wasn't paying any attention to them; instead, she focused all of her energy on a small group of trees. The two wolves raced into that stand of conifers. Soon, a cow elk came running out with the wolves right behind her and closing ground. The elk, in poor condition, was soon brought down by 755 and 889. Despite all the elk tracks and scents in that area, 889 had been able to detect that there was one unhealthy elk—a relatively easy kill.

And yet, 755's bad luck continued. The new mates were outside the park boundary on December 10 when 889 was shot and wounded. She had been hit in the right front leg. The injury was serious enough to leave her hobbled, but it appeared she would survive. In the early days of January 2014, the pair were hunting elk, with 889 running on three legs after one herd while 755 pursued a different group. When he was able to catch and attack a cow elk, 889 rushed to him and helped finish off the animal. It was an impressive effort from a wolf still getting over a gunshot wound.

Back in Lamar Valley, the tiny remnant of the Lamar pack got still smaller when Middle Gray mysteriously disappeared, leaving only the two alphas, 925 and 926.

February 6, 2014, was the coldest day I had ever experienced in Yellowstone—or anywhere else. Several of us had stopped to watch the Lamar wolves, 925 and 926, up at the den forest. One man had a thermometer that registered a temperature of -55 degrees Fahrenheit (-48 degrees Celsius). The wolves were comfortably resting and seemed unaffected by the extreme cold. I was not as tough as them and had to go back to my car to warm up.

★ RICK

◇ ◇ ◇

February brought mating season, and the two alpha Lamars were clearly enjoying each other—romping, playfighting, and hunting together. Their bond was growing stronger, and they were becoming a Yellowstone power couple. They were also spending a lot of time in the

Druid den forest area. It was beginning to look like 926, if she was pregnant, would have her pups in the same den forest where her grandmother 472 had been born and where her mother, 06, had denned. Druid litters had been born in that area dating all the way back to 1997.

On an especially chilly day in February 2014, 926 caught and killed a beaver. Wolves rarely had much success hunting beavers, but 926 had surprised this one and caught it before it could slip underwater. She ate the tail first. A beaver's tail, rich in stored fat, is a delicacy for wolves, and 926 clearly didn't intend to share that part of her prize with her mate. But the rest of that beaver carcass (which likely weighed anywhere from 30 to 60 pounds or about 14 to 27 kilograms) would provide several meals for the two Lamars.

In March, 926 started spending more time underground in the den itself. She was three years old and about to be a first-time mother, though she had helped her mother and older sister with their pups. By the end of April, she was staying in the den, an indication to park staff that she might have had her pups.

While 926 was welcoming her first litter, 755's misfortunes continued. Wolf 889 had been pregnant, but it quickly became evident that none of the pups had survived. Two years had now passed without him siring a litter. He had mated with 759, but she had been killed, and now 889 had been unsuccessful with this litter, perhaps because of the long-term effects of her injury. Following that failure, 889 and 755 seemed to be spending a lot more time apart. While 889 was frequently spotted traveling on or near the road, often near cars and people, 755 wasn't comfortable with human contact. Eventually, the two of them just drifted apart.

The Lamar alpha pair, on the other hand, were doing just fine. 925 went on regular hunts, then returned to feed the new mother wolf. On one occasion he carried half of a dead bison calf all the way back to the den, a distance of 4 miles (about 6.5 kilometers).

It wasn't until July 10 that the pups followed their mother out of the den forest for the first time. There were six blacks and one gray, seven in all. It was a big day, not only for the proud parents and the pups, but for all the people who had cared so much about Wolf 06. Her daughter was carrying on the legacy of strong female wolves that had been 06's trademark.

In August of that year, with the pups now a few months old (there were six remaining, as one of the black pups had not survived), 926 was taking the family to the Chalcedony rendezvous site, where the pups could safely explore and play. In order to get to that spot, however, they would have to cross a road. 926 showed her resourcefulness by traveling with a bone in her mouth. She would drop it from time to time, and when a pup went to grab it, she would pick it up and run off with it. In this way, she was using the bone as a lure to get the pups to follow her.

Years before, the famed Druid female Wolf 42 had used the same strategy with a stick to get her pups to follow her. It was a trick smart mothers used with their young, and 926 was a smart mother wolf.

Seeing 926 with her pups caused me to think about her father. On July 21, we had a major sighting. I drove down to Hayden Valley, a large region of open territory in the center of Yellowstone, and saw 755 with a young, light gray Canyon pack female. They traveled north with her in the lead, and I lost them going into a forest. The following day I saw them flirting with each other. She went to him with a wagging tail and jumped on his rear end. Later she licked his face as he wagged his tail. 755 had spent the year and a half since the death of 06 looking for a suitable partner. I had a feeling this female was the one he was destined to be with. He did pair off with her, but since it was long past the mating season, they would have to wait until next year to have pups. ★ RICK

926 and her family stayed at the rendezvous area through the summer and into the fall, and then moved to the Chalcedony Creek area, a centrally located meadow the Druids had used as a rendezvous site for generations. Late in October, the Lamars were in pursuit of

a massive bull elk. 925 got hold of a back leg while 926 tried to get in front to attack the bull from there. The bull lowered his head and charged at 926, but 925 hung on to the back leg, causing the bull to miss his mate. 926 joined 925 and bit into the bull's hindquarters. While all this was going on, the pups were jumping around excitedly. They didn't really know how to help and seemed afraid to make contact with this very large animal that was fighting and kicking. Finally, the two alphas managed to bring the elk down in a patch of thick sage. The pups moved in then and bit at the struggling bull. The elk soon died. This kill had been a huge learning experience for the pups, as they were able to help with the final moments of the hunt.

A few days later a grizzly came near the pack. First a black pup approached the bear, and then the rest of the Lamars joined in. 925 bit the bear on the hind end, and the pack harassed the animal until it finally wandered off. A few days later, though, the same bear returned. This time, the pups greeted the grizzly like a long-lost friend. The bear and the wolves then traveled together, with the bear in the middle of the group surrounded by the wolves. The bear didn't bother the wolves, and none of the wolves harassed the bear. It seemed they had settled on a peace treaty that worked for both sides.

On a cold December day, twelve Mollie's arrived in Lamar Valley. The group included six pups and their new alpha male, an uncollared gray. They howled and were answered by several members of the Junction Butte pack. The Mollie's moved off to the north, apparently wanting to avoid conflict, a very different attitude from when the violent 686 was the alpha female and leader of that pack.

The next morning it was the Lamars that set up a howl. The Mollie's and some of the Junctions howled back. A black pup from the Junctions got separated from its pack. It became disoriented and started running toward the Lamars, apparently thinking they were its family. 926 and the rest of the Lamars charged at the pup, recalling the siege of their denning area by the Mollie's a few years before. The Junction pup, who now realized its mistake, turned and ran away. 926 easily caught the pup and pulled it down. It squirmed away and ran off again, but 926 caught it a second time and bit it a few times—though not hard enough to do much harm. This time when the pup escaped, she let it go. This showed that 926 had a forgiving attitude when it came to pups from another pack.

The Mollie's wolves soon left the valley without causing any problems for 926 and her family. It appeared that, just maybe, the long-standing feud between the Lamars and the Mollie's had finally been laid to rest. 926's decision to spare the life of the Mollie's pup may well have been the reason the two packs stopped fighting with one another.

There were, however, four other wolves in the area that day, members of the Prospect Peak pack that had been denning to the west at Blacktail Plateau. It would not be the last time the Prospect wolves and the Lamars would encounter one another—and the next time would be much more dramatic.

10

Hard Times

The year 2015 marked the celebration of a significant milestone: Exactly twenty years had passed since the arrival of the first three wolf packs from Alberta, Canada, as part of the Yellowstone Wolf Reintroduction Project, widely regarded as the most successful wildlife reintroduction ever undertaken.

But for the Yellowstone wolves of 2015, it was pretty much business as usual. 926 was enjoying motherhood, spending time playing with her pups. In that way she was very much like her great-grandfather, Wolf 21, who had loved spending time playing with his pups and teaching them the skills they would need to be successful adult wolves.

February was mating season, and 926 and 925 soon started trying for their next litter of pups. But things didn't always go smoothly. One time, the two had entered into the mating tie—the way wolves breed—but

926 wasn't entirely focused. While still in the tie, she started dragging her mate toward a carcass the family had been feeding on. When they got there, 926 began feeding while the mating process continued. When 925 finally completed his task, the pair broke apart and he was able to feed, too.

Several days later, the pack was hunting together. The 2014 pups, not quite yearlings, were quickly learning the techniques of the hunt. While most of the Lamars were pursuing a large group of elk, 926 and one of the pups were tracking a subgroup of three elk cows and had followed them to the top of a cliff. 926 approached one of the cows at the very edge of the drop-off and grabbed hold of a back leg. 926 was able to wrestle the cow to the ground, but it was able to get free and stand up again. Now unstable on that sore leg, the cow backed too near the cliff's edge, eventually toppling over and tumbling to the ground far below. 926 raced down to the base of the cliff and was soon feeding on the elk carcass. She eventually rejoined the rest of her family, but one of the pups was able to get the scent of the dead elk cow on 926's coat and worked its way down to the carcass on its own. Soon the rest of the Lamars joined the adventurous pup, and all of them fed on the elk.

Mating season brought exciting news to the members of the wolf project. All of them had been hoping that 755 would at last find the right female to start a new pack, after the tragedies of losing 06 and a couple of other potential mates. And finally, things were looking up for the wolf who had been such an amazing partner to 06 for so long. He and the light gray female had mated in February, and that April the female had a litter of four pups in the Hayden Valley part of Yellowstone. The new family would be called the Wapiti Lake pack. The name was especially fitting, as *wapiti* is a Shawnee and Cree word for elk.

The Prospect Peak wolves, who had been in Lamar Valley a few months before, were now denning on the Blacktail Plateau. They numbered fourteen. They were a violent pack, much like the Mollie's had been when 686 was the alpha female. On March 6, a large group of Prospect wolves were feeding on a carcass near Slough Creek, adjacent to Lamar Valley. The Lamars were off to the west, coming back from feeding on the elk that had died after falling from the cliff. 925 was in the lead and 926 was at the back of the line, with the eleven-month-old pups in between.

When the wolves came through a pass and saw the Prospects, 926 did the smart thing. She turned and fled back to the west. The pups were well trained and took off after their mother. By that time the other wolves had spotted the family and were running toward them. 925 did not move. He stood facing the onslaught of charging

Prospects and finally, at the last minute, raced off to the east, in a different direction than that taken by the rest of his family.

All of the Prospects pursued him, and even though he ran as hard as he could, they eventually caught up with him and pulled him down. The attack continued for several minutes, until a group of the Lamar pups appeared on a nearby ridge and howled. That momentarily distracted the Prospects, and they took off in the direction of the pups. But they soon decided to return to where they'd left 925, likely to finish him off. When they got there, however, the Lamar alpha male was gone. A black Prospect pup picked up 925's scent and followed him. 925 was in rough shape, bleeding from several parts of his body and limping badly on one injured leg. The pup caught up and bit 925 on the injured leg, but 925 was able to drive off the young attacker and continue to move away from the rest of the Prospects.

The Lamar alpha male had put his life on the line for his family. He knew that his mate was pregnant and would be unable to fight or run very fast. 925 had stood his ground so the rival wolves would attack him, allowing 926 and the young Lamars to escape. He had paid a heavy price for his bravery, and the question now was whether he'd be able to survive the severe injuries the rival pack had inflicted on him.

Later that day, 926 found 925 lying not far from where the attack occurred. She licked his face and some of his wounds. He was in great pain, and she knew he would not be able to get up and follow her back to the pups. After a couple more licks, she began to leave. But before she left, she stopped and looked back at her mate. It was the last time they would be together. Not long after she left, 925 took his last breath, knowing that his sacrifice had been worth it. His mate and the pups he had sired were all safe—and they were safe because of him.

926 understood that their time together had ended. She was going to have to look after her family all by herself.

I felt 06 had picked the right two males to help her form a pack, males she could rely on in a dangerous crisis like the den raid. Now events proved that her daughter had also picked the right mate, for he died heroically protecting 926 and her pups. ★ RICK

11

The 06 Legend Lives On

926 had an immediate and very serious problem. She had a family of young wolves and was due to have another litter in just a few weeks. And she was now a single mom, with no male partner to help protect the family from danger, provide meat for her growing pups, and, most importantly, offer the support she needed when she was in the den giving birth to pups.

She took her family to the carcass the Prospect wolves had been feeding on before the attack that claimed the life of 925. Then she led the pups to the spot where he had died. They stayed at that spot a while, sniffing, walking back and forth, and grieving the loss of their father. A couple of days later, 926 took down a mule deer, vital to the feeding and nourishment of the six sons and daughters she was caring for and also important for her. She would need to maintain a strong, healthy body to handle the physical challenges ahead.

On March 22, the situation took what looked like a turn for the worse. 926 and her pups were in two separate groups. Three of the pups were with her and the other three were in a second group heading to the east, quite a distance from their mom and siblings. What made matters look especially dire was the presence of three Prospect wolves positioned between the two Lamar groups. The Prospect males were Wolf 965, his brother, who was uncollared and had been given the name Twin by wolf project staff, and another uncollared wolf, this one called Mottled Black.

These were the wolves responsible for the death of 925. Had they come back to finish the job and eliminate the Lamars completely? 926 considered the situation and made a decision—one that was both brilliant and necessary, but also very dangerous. She approached the biggest Prospect male, Twin, wagged her tail, and greeted him in a friendly manner. Twin responded with a cordial, almost affectionate response. A fourth Prospect male now joined the group, and all of them seemed very much intrigued by this interesting female.

At first the pups seemed afraid of the large Prospect males, which was not surprising since just days earlier they had killed their father. The pups kept well away from the newcomers. Eventually, though, Twin led the adults to the pups. 926 took over the lead position, and the four males behaved in a friendly manner toward the pups. They reached one of the young females and greeted her gently. Meanwhile, 926 flirted with each of the four males in turn, and the Prospects responded with the tender behavior they'd shown since getting closer to her.

But that wasn't the end of 926's charming ways. Within a few days, not only had she won them over but she had also established herself as the leader of the group, even though she was the smallest of the adults. Because 926 was the alpha female, the pack would continue with the name the Lamar Canyon pack.

It was a remarkable accomplishment by a very resourceful female. In a matter of days she had taken a group of aggressive males—wolves that had killed her mate, no less—and converted them from enemies to support staff.

Despite the fact that Twin and the other Prospect males seemed to be accepting the Lamar pups, the pups themselves—five in total now—still seemed traumatized by the presence of the wolves that had killed their father. The young Lamars stayed away from 926 and the male wolves. Eventually, the pups left Lamar Valley and headed west, perhaps to try to establish a pack of their own.

Right around that time, a large group of Mollie's appeared in the valley and did some howling. Twin, who had established himself as the alpha male for the new group of wolves, and two of the other Prospect wolves howled back. Despite their superior numbers, the Mollie's wanted nothing to do with the four big, strong males who had now become part of a pack with 926 as their leader. It was clear that 926 had chosen wisely in forming her alliance with the Prospect wolves. They would serve as more than adequate protectors for a female who was about to have pups. And although 925 had fathered the yet-unborn pups, it would be the Prospect males who would help raise them.

In late April, 926 disappeared into her den to prepare it for the arrival of the pups. She came out a couple of days later to quickly feed on a fresh elk kill, and then went directly back up the hill to her den. The next morning she and Twin were back at the elk carcass. While 926 fed on the carcass, Twin walked around the area, waiting his turn. But he was also watching, looking first in one direction, then in another. He was keeping an eye out for possible threats to 926. She grabbed a large piece of meat and carried it up to the den. Only then did Twin feed. Afterward, he went back to the den, still on active guard duty.

In early May, all four of the Prospect males were taking turns looking after 926, guarding the den area while she was inside and bringing meat to her as well. A few days after her pups were born, she was strong enough to leave the den and travel several miles to get to food sources.

926's dominance over her male companions was very much in evidence almost every day. On one spring morning, she casually ate her fill of a bison carcass while three of the Prospect males were patiently bedded down nearby to await their turn. A couple of days later, at another carcass, 926 and Twin got into a dispute, and the big male ended up on his back in the defeated position—more evidence that in this family, as in all wolf families, the alpha female is dominant to the alpha male.

When 926 and the Prospect males encountered a mountain lion at a freshly killed elk carcass, it was the alpha female who put the run on the cat and chased it up a tree. None of the males offered any help during the chase. Instead, they raced over to the carcass and stuffed themselves while 926 was dealing with the cat.

During that spring two of the Lamar females who had left with the rest of the young wolves returned. Because they were females, they likely felt safer with the group that included 926 and four male Prospects. They weren't competition for the males and, even more important, they could soon be bred and add more litters of pups to the newly reorganized pack. One of those two females who returned to the pack would eventually succeed her mother as the next Lamar alpha female.

926 had five pups in her litter that year. The summer was a time of growth, learning, and, of course, play. On a bright end of a July afternoon, the five pups

were enjoying an especially good day. After pestering one of the yearling females into regurgitating food for them, they chased each other, then had a three-way tug-of-war over a stick. Later, one of them appeared to be hiding behind a tree, peeking out one side, then the other—the wolf version of hide-and-seek. 926 and the adults howled, and then the pups joined in.

That healthy, active family at play was a perfect illustration of the resilience of female wolves. 926 had gone through some tough times. First, she had lost her uncle and faithful friend, 754, and her mother, 06, to hunters. Her father, 755, left the family to find a new mate. Later, her mate, 925, gave up his life to save the members of his family. But through all of that 926 had persevered, finally recruiting four males to her family and then having a healthy litter.

926 had been watching her family on that day. She was likely feeling proud—certainly of them but also of herself. Despite all of the losses and tragedies that had been thrown at her, despite the almost overwhelming challenges, she had never given up.

While 926 was giving birth to and then nursing her pups, the yearling Lamar wolves had traveled well outside the park boundary, which meant that they were in danger due to the legal wolf-hunting season that would take place in the area come fall. But just a few days later, with fall still

a long way off, a young black male was shot and killed. An investigation was immediately underway.

That dead wolf that had been found north of the park turned out to be one of the Lamar yearlings, and it had been illegally shot. Whoever killed him had left the body to rot. That shooting was a hard thing for those of us who knew that wolf's family. The pack had endured so many tragedies: the shootings of 754 and 06, and then the loss of 925. The killing of that yearling was one death too many for me.

I began to doubt if the thousands of wolf talks I did for park visitors were having much of an impact. I believed in the power of the stories about the Yellowstone wolves, especially the ones about 8, 21, 42, 306, 06, 925, and 926. But were those stories making any real difference? Was everything I and so many other people had done to share their stories in vain?

Then there was a day that seemed like it was going to be the worst of my career. I had been asked to give a talk to some schoolchildren who lived in a town with many residents known to be very anti-wolf. I had never had a problem speaking in such situations, but this time was different.

After the teacher introduced me, but before I could start to talk, a kindergarten boy, probably five years old spoke up: "I know the man that shot that famous wolf," he told me. The killing of Wolf 06 was still a big story in the region, and I knew he had to be talking about her.

I could not think of a proper response. As far as we knew the shooting had been done legally, so, as a national park ranger in uniform, I could not voice an opinion about wolf-hunting regulations outside of the park. Having been a five-year-old boy myself, I could understand how this boy might have a heroic image of the man who'd killed the famous wolf.

I figured I would just start telling stories of the wolves I had known in Yellowstone and hope they might have some impact on these kids, especially that boy. But before I could begin, he spoke up again. He looked straight at me and said, "My dad just bought a license to kill a wolf!"

Now I was really stuck. I couldn't think of anything to say that would not make the situation worse. There was only one way out. I was about to say "I need to start my talk, so no more questions or comments," but before I had a chance the boy spoke for the third time.

His first two words were "I hope..." and then there was a brief pause. I guessed what he was about to say. "I hope he gets a big one" or, even worse, "I hope I get to kill a wolf someday."

But then he finished his sentence. He said, "... I hope he doesn't."

As far as I knew, that boy had grown up hearing frequent negative comments about wolves from the adults around him. But something had happened that caused him to reject that view. I think it was the story of 06's life. Perhaps it was his teacher giving a lesson on wolves. Or maybe it was the Bob Landis documentary on 06. That film was a big hit that played frequently on television. He had likely seen it, perhaps many times. I felt that 06's story had connected with that boy and changed him, and he wanted to tell me that he hoped his father would not kill a wolf.

That moment had a deep impact on me. It gave me renewed hope in the power of stories about wolves to reach people and change them. And it led me to finishing up with the National Park Service so I could devote myself to writing books about the Yellowstone wolves. For years they allowed me to watch their lives, to see their pups grow up, find mates, and start families of their own through many generations. I saw them in their good times and their hard times. Most importantly, I learned their stories. And it was time to write those stories down so I could share them with everyone. No one ever truly leaves us as long as we keep on telling their story. ★ RICK

About the Authors

RICK MCINTYRE has spent more time observing and documenting wolves in the wild than any other person. A retired National Park Service ranger and wolf researcher, Rick has watched wolves in America's national parks for forty-six years, thirty of those in Yellowstone, where he has accumulated over 100,000 wolf sightings, worked on the Yellowstone Wolf Reintroduction Project, and educated the public about the park's wolves, including by writing several books for adult readers (*The Rise of Wolf 8*, *The Reign of Wolf 21*, *The Redemption of Wolf 302*, *The Alpha Female Wolf*, *Thinking Like a Wolf*, and *My Life With Wolves*). He lives in Silver Gate, Montana. To learn more about him and his books, visit rickmcintyrebooks.com.

DAVID A. POULSEN is the author of thirty-four books, many of them for middle readers. His young adult novel *Numbers* was selected for the Sakura Medal (awarded by English-speaking high school students in Japan to their favorite novel of the year). His teen/young adult novel *And Then the Sky Exploded* was a nominee for the 2018 Ontario Library Association's Red Maple Award. He divides his time between Saskatoon, Saskatchewan; Maricopa, Arizona; and Claresholm, Alberta. To learn more about David and his work, visit davidapoulsenauthor.com.

26 27 28 29 30 5 4 3 2 1

Greystone Kids / Greystone Books Ltd.
greystonebooks.com

Cataloguing data available from Library and Archives Canada
ISBN 978-1-77840-195-4 (cloth)
ISBN 978-1-77840-196-1 (epub)

Editing by Linda Pruessen
Copy editing by Tracy Bordian
Proofreading by Alison Strobel
Cover and interior design by Jessica Sullivan | DSGN Dept.
Cover illustration by Lieke van der Vorst
Interior illustrations by John Potter

Printed and bound in Canada on FSC® certified paper at Friesens. The FSC® label means that materials used for the product have been responsibly sourced.

Greystone Books thanks the Canada Council for the Arts, the British Columbia Arts Council, the Province of British Columbia through the Book Publishing Tax Credit, and the Government of Canada for supporting our publishing activities.

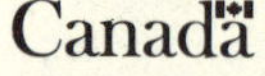

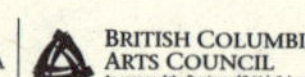

EU Safety Information: Easy Access System Europe, Mustamäe tee 50, 10621 Tallinn, Estonia, gpsr.requests@easproject.com.

Greystone Books gratefully acknowledges the xʷməθkʷəy̓əm (Musqueam), Sḵwx̱wú7mesh (Squamish), and səlilwətaɬ (Tsleil-Waututh) peoples on whose land our Vancouver head office is located.